Dog

Animal
Series editor: Jonathan Burt

Already published

Crow
Boria Sax

Tortoise
Peter Young

Cockroach
Marion Copeland

Ant
Charlotte Sleigh

Oyster
Rebecca Stott

Forthcoming

Rat
Jonathan Burt

Wolf
Garry Marvin

Snake
Drake Stutesman

Falcon
Helen Macdonald

Dog

Susan McHugh

REAKTION BOOKS

For Mik

Published by

REAKTION BOOKS LTD

79 Farringdon Road

London EC1M 3JU, UK

www.reaktionbooks.co.uk

First published 2004

Copyright © Susan McHugh 2004

Printed in China

British Library Cataloguing in Publication Data

McHugh, Susan
    Dog. – (Animal)
    1. Dogs 2. Dogs – History 3. Animals and civilization
    I. Title
    636.7'009

ISBN 1 86189 203 9

Contents

Jean-Léon Gérôme, *Study of a Newfoundland Dog*, 1852, oil on canvas.

1 Canine Beginnings

The problem facing everyone who writes about dogs is that there are thousands, if not millions, of people who have already done so. Like dogs themselves, dog literature abounds and, in part because of this wealth of materials, dog books tend to lose in coherence what they gain in comprehensiveness. In attempting to reconcile too much information, such texts take on a randomness that even those of us who call ourselves 'dog people' find tedious. Predictably, these documents of dogs frustrate even the most comprehensive attempts at categorization, and threaten to rub our noses in the mess we make of understanding dogs. But in their chaos they also remain faithful to our confusing (sometimes confused) experiences with canine companions. The difficulty of representing dogs – let alone accounting for how they have become a central part of the human experience – reflects the ongoing struggle of defining what a dog is.

Narrowing the subject to the most familiar kind, domesticated dogs or *Canis familiaris*, helps only slightly. This group of animals has the largest range of body types and sizes of any mammal, ranging anywhere from 0.5 to 100 kilos (1 to 250 lb), any combination of which can produce fertile offspring; the broadest geographic range of all four-footed creatures (their populations are second only to humans in worldwide distribution); the longest history of human domestication of any

Is Your Big Dog Looking For A Bigger Snack?

animal by several thousand years; and the ability to produce fertile offspring with other species, including coyotes, jackals and wolves. (This last quality famously led Charles Darwin to despair of ever ascertaining 'with certainty' the origin of this particular species.[1]) Taken together, the wide-ranging morphology, distribution, history and reproductive physiology of the dog boggle the human imagination.

But if these qualities hinder definitive representations of dogs they also secure room for play in the process of representing them. The size differences between familiar breeds such as chihuahuas and Great Danes, for instance, enable a dog-eat-dog visual pun in a current ad for Jumbone dog snacks; the ad implies that if you don't do your part as a consumer, then your big dog might literally consume a smaller one. More subtly, the ad presents a product that itself attests to the decisive role of mass marketing in the long history of canine adaptation to human cohabitation. A descendent of the first commercially prepared food specifically marketed for pets – a dog biscuit introduced 150 years ago in Britain – the dog snack ad also figures a shared modern history in which the dog moves from primarily working animal to pet. Although such uses of dogs have become so common as to seem banal, they clearly draw from the same canine complexity that has inspired the human imagination to forge new modes and methods of expression, across thousands of years and in nearly every corner of the world. If their chaotic omnipresence causes headaches for librarians and researchers, it also ensures the central cultural work of dogs in complicating rather than resolving questions of representation.

Reflecting an enormous range of social practices, the material evidence of dogs in our lives, though daunting, becomes all the more compelling even for non-'doggy people' – those who do not put their trust in dogs[2] – when considering how it corresponds directly to large populations of these creatures. Since their archives as a whole are but poorly understood, dogs themselves must suffer from our confused and conflicted understanding of their significance. The dangers for contemporary dogs are real: destroyed by the millions every year as unwanted pets, strays and research subjects, domesticated dogs bear the double-bind of sharing many of the maladies as well as the joys of living the so-called good life, and they are also subjected to the mass killings that the world's poorest people and the majority of all animal species now suffer on an unprecedented scale. Intersecting with humans' ideas of each other, the long histories of conflicting attitudes towards dogs illuminate these lived contradictions.

No dogs crystallize this ambivalence more distinctly than those of the Walt Disney pantheon, a feeling that comes to the fore in the childhood conundrum: if Pluto is Mickey Mouse's dog, then what on earth is Goofy? Silly in its usual playground context, this question also pairs these global icons as bookends to a range of contemporary attitudes toward dogs. On the one end there is Pluto, the faithful and beloved pet, whose Classical name and quintessentially silent and sympathetic character secure his 'privileged' status as a 'personified animal'. And on the other end is Goofy, the daft and bumbling sidekick who, in spite of all the privileges of language, tools and even two-legged walking ability, strays far from the ideals of human or dog. At worst reviled or 'despised', even Goofy's appeal remains that of a 'degraded human',[3] a criticism both unselfconsciously and ironically applied to dogs. Seen as a comic grotesque, Goofy is

Cartoon from *49 Dogs, 36 Cats, & A Platypus* (1999).

"ANTHROPOMORPHISM — THAT'S WHERE THE MONEY IS."

akin to the stock 'animal' characters of American blackface minstrelsy such as Zip Coon, which were rapidly being relocated from stage to cartoon at the time of their inception. Today, as Disney products find markets across the world, these interlocked extremes – Goofy's Rover and Pluto's Fido – not only evoke strong emotions about dogs but also bear histories of cultural differences that colour viewers' relationships with other animals as well as each other.

Fortunately, the omnipresence of the canine race inspires constant scrutiny of these ideas as well. Both clothed clown and naked mute, the fluctuating dog in this doubled Disney vision is a testament to the creation and malleability of canine archetypes: in the twentieth century Fido became an acronym both for flawed coins and fog-dispersal systems, while Rover became the first canine film star and a popular pet name through the film of 1904, *Rescued by Rover*. Together, these extreme characterizations serve as a powerful object lesson in anthropomorphism, of the projection of ideas of the human into animal bodies. But their ongoing rebirth in Disney dog characters – *The Shaggy Dog*, *101 Dalmations*, *Air Bud* – serialized and remade, decade after decade, in turn reflects the inherent instability of the natural and cultural status of not only animals but also humans. Goofy and Pluto may lead the pack of popular dog characters, but they do not simply reflect or instil stable hierarchies of social difference. Often such characters even inspire critiques of existing social relationships as well as help us to imagine new ones.

To gain insight into how dogs gain this pivotal position, this book poses some questions about historic approaches to writing and thinking about dogs, tracing how and when dogs operate as aesthetic, sexual and scientific objects as well as paying close attention to the more rarefied moments when dogs contribute

A still from Charles Barton's 1959 film *The Shaggy Dog*.

to historic transformations in society and culture. This chapter focuses specifically on the contested beginnings, namely the emergence of these most familiar canids at the dawn of human civilization, to show how conflicting theories of their biological origins intersect with broader philosophical and linguistic approaches to defining dogs. As an animal that emerges between (and sometimes interbreeds with) others, the dog presents special challenges to species-centred notions of history. Consequently, the various canine origin myths across the arts and sciences highlight not just the problems of dogs' placement within taxonomies. Although it may be easy to accept that popular cultural representations of dogs are purposeful distortions of some natural, common-sense reality, these in turn stem from a construction of this very 'nature' of dogs that traces specific conflicts of and within human cultures throughout recorded time.

As is the case with the human, the very definition of the dog is at stake in scientific attempts to date the origin of the species.

Theodore of
Caesarea, 'David
the Shepherd'
(Psalm 26) from
the 11th-century
Byzantine
Theodore Psalter.

Recent genetic studies, attempting to account for the similarities
of dogs to (and patterns of interbreeding with) other species,
suggest that *Canis familiaris* dates back as far as 500,000 years.[4]
Conclusions from these studies are complicated, however, by
dogs' reproductive anomalies. Wolves, jackals and coyotes have
interbred with dogs in irretrievable patterns across thousands of
years, making these populations too intermixed to support a
straightforward, linear story of the descent of dogs from one

species.[5] Although genetic methods have proved helpful in tracing relatively homogenous species, *Canis familiaris* remains the nexus of diversity within the canid group, a veritable biological wonder for its ranges of physical diversity achieved so rapidly.[6] Exactly how the mixed-species genetic heritage of dogs influences these aspects remains uncertain.

Even the results of studies that track mitochondrial DNA (mtDNA), genetic material that passes virtually unchanged from mother to daughter, can be used to support oppositional theories. For instance, the anthropologist Janice Koler-Matznick concluded that these data justify a reclassification of wolves and dogs as the same species,[7] a concept proposed by the eighteenth-century taxonomer John Hunter but rejected by his more famous contemporary Carl Linnaeus, who designated the dog a separate species because of its upturned tail in the two-name system (*Canis familiaris, Homo sapiens*, etc.) that has since became the dominant method of biological classification.[8] More recently, Raymond Coppinger and Richard Schneider have suggested that the new genetic research makes wolves start to look like another breed of dog,[9] an idea corroborated by the wolf ecologist L. David Mech, who asserts that the wolf 'is a large wild dog'.[10] These latter approaches develop the Darwinian concept of adaptation as speciation, insisting that all canids descend from 'wolf-like' (pointedly not 'wolf') ancestors.

These contested species definitions of 'dog' thus illuminate a larger struggle within biology over how to define 'species', whether morphologically (according to measurable differences) or ecologically (according to adaptation to a specific environment). The Linnaean system, premised on creationism, shares with most Darwinian approaches the idea that a species has a distinct physical type.[11] For endangered canids, the political consequences of these hypotheses can be devastating. Relatively

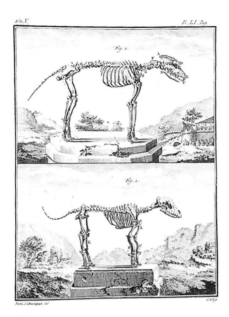

A dog skeleton, from the Amsterdam edition of Buffon and Daubenton's *Histoire naturelle* (1766–99).

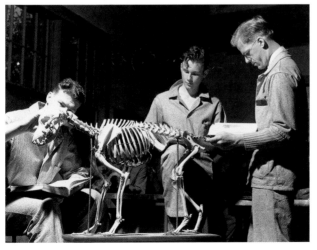

Students with the skeleton of a dog in a veterinary school anatomy class at Iowa State College, Ames, 1942.

isolated for several thousand years, Australian dingo populations have been radically reduced within the past few hundred years both by Western settlers, who exterminate them as a livestock menace, and by feral European-type dogs, who interbreed with them. The case for ecological protection can be made only for distinct species that can be definitively measured as well as socially valued, so the dingo's recent reclassification as a sub-species of dog – now both its greatest threat and closest relative – puts the very definition of dog on the front lines of this debate.[12]

Because of this long history of defining species through physical form, the origins of dogs have typically been traced through the archaeological evidence of dog remains in human burial sites. These date the emergence of the dog as a distinct species to 12,000 to 14,000 years ago, during the last Ice Age. And the strong appeal of this dating system reflects both the special status of dogs as the first domesticated animals and their conventional roles as human companions. In these origin stories, dogs and humans together made the crucial transition from nomadic hunter-gatherer to settled agricultural life as the ice receded. Thus set in the foundations of human history, in these accounts the origins of dogs – like dogs themselves – appear inseparable from those of contemporary human cultures.

These bones, interred with human skeletons, suggest that dogs were present within human cultures throughout this archaeologically significant period of transition, from the palaeolithic to the neolithic periods. In Oberkassel, Germany, the oldest of such sites evinces a society whose hunting technologies 14,000 years ago were rapidly becoming more precise; these people were then replacing heavy, stone-throwing axes that crushed prey with more precise, stone-bladed arrows that could more easily mortally wound it. While the contributions

Paolo Veronese, *Boy with a Greyhound*, c. 1570, oil on canvas.

of dogs to the development of new hunting strategies remain a matter of speculation, the long-term effects of such changes have been unequivocal.

Multiple sites in Palestine dating back 12,000 years show humans who lived in stone dwellings interred with dogs in stone-covered tombs. Examples include one elderly woman with a hand on the thorax of a puppy and another person buried with two adult dogs. Dated within a few thousand years of the Israeli site, similar remains considered to be of early dogs have been unearthed not only in this area but also around the world, in China, Iraq and Chile.[13] Many of these dogs are believed to be burial sacrifices, in part because the use of dogs as burial gifts continued in Europe through early medieval times.[14] This association of dogs with death continued symbolically with depictions of dogs at the feet of their masters in tombs, and more recently with public monuments to dead dogs. Taken together, such evidence establishes how dogs flourish in human company at the same time that it raises questions about how these relationships define these species.

Because global populations plummeted at the onset of this great climactic shift, fossil evidence for all species from the period remains rare, a chronic complication of all archaeological theories of origins. Whole skulls of early dogs are extremely rare[15] and easily confused with smaller, now extinct wolf species.[16] The common pattern of defining canid differences physically, in terms of sometimes-miniscule reductions in head, brain and tooth size,[17] makes classification even more problematic. In lieu of these murky physical distinctions, what counts as 'dog' in the fossil evidence has been determined less by precise definitions of dog remains and more by their proximity to signs of human settlement. In other words, the current archaeological agreement about the origin of dogs rests not on the material evidence of a

Dogs in Godhavn, Greenland: 'Some of the dogs belonging to the household are nearly always asleep on top of the huts and this makes the huts look still more like mounds of grass' wrote Josephine Diebitsch Peary in *Children of the Arctic* (1903).

species evolving distinct physical characteristics (morphology) but on the circumstantial evidence of humans and dogs evolving a cross-species relationship (ecology). Comparison of archaeological sites dating from the period creates a story within which the origins of dogs paradoxically coincide with their becoming part of everyday human life, a story that resonates with mythological and material evidence that the dog has shared in the development of human civilizations throughout the world. As recently as the time of contact with Europeans, dogs were the only domestic animals living within the majority of Native American and Australian Aboriginal groups,[18] a circumstance that highlights how dogs provide primary connections across animal and human worlds.

Dogs seem unthinkable outside the context of human culture and, what is more, culture as we know it has been inseparable from their presence. But accurately accounting for such canine complexity has proved a profound challenge for scientists. As the genetic debates about the dog–wolf species distinctions suggest, biological origin stories of the dog have frequently been based on comparison with other contemporary animals, and these tales quickly morph into depictions of dogs as their 'tame' descendents. While the ability of dogs to interbreed with several other animals gives the lie to these myths – historically tying lines of descent into a Gordian knot – for many people this cross-species heritage has become an opportunity to claim just the opposite: that the shifting category 'dog' becomes stabilized when connected backwards to a non-domesticated species, usually the wolf. Although it is equally plausible that wolves and dogs share ancestry in a common but now extinct species, such a story challenges the ideological value of dogs as role models for 'naturally' exploited animals or inevitably inferior humans. Pluto and Goofy are not so easily forgotten.

In spite of these favourable social conditions, scientific evidence supporting the idea that the dog is 'essentially a debased and corrupted wolf'[19] remains controversial. Before their widespread extermination by humans, wolves held the distinction of being the most broadly distributed four-footed animal, a position subsequently assumed by dogs. Fossil evidence of their common worldwide dispersal confirms that wolves and dogs initially shared habitats with humans. Again, exactly how these proximities or environmental pressures shaped the development of each species remains uncertain. What is clear, however, is that profound differences in some behaviour and morphology, as well as compelling overlaps in other behaviour and genetics, plague the notion that the dog is simply a domesticated version of the few remaining wolves left today.

Today there are at least 4,000 dogs for every wolf, a vast difference in extant populations between a tiny group of wolves and a burgeoning mass of dogs that makes them nearly impossible to compare. Even in an extreme situation such as mainland China, where the Cultural Revolution of the mid-twentieth century led to the systematic slaughter or banishment of almost half a million dogs from Beijing alone, dogs have been maintained under special circumstances as police dogs, laboratory research animals, livestock (or dogs kept as food) and guards. In rare circumstances, dogs have been kept as the pets of privileged officials, a sentimental human–dog relationship that has been traditionally alien to the ordinary workers of China.[20] One such official, an American diplomat stationed in Beijing in the early 1970s, remembers incredulous Chinese children who saw a closer similarity between her pet cocker spaniel and cats than to the hound-like dogs that remained primarily outside the cities.[21] In this extreme situation, even people with no experience of dogs in their everyday lives still express distinct notions about what a dog should look like and how it should behave.

The wolf may be more readily recognizable to the naked eye but is rarely seen. Little is known of wolf behaviour outside captivity. Like wild dogs, wolves shun human observation, and this trait, combined with their scarcity, has made it impossible to obtain detailed information about their behaviour.[22] Field studies that document some wolf interactions with each other and the worlds around them show that the animals behave in ways that are consistently different from dogs. Given hunting opportunities, for instance, they do not choose to survive on human rubbish, as do some foxes, jackals, coyotes and all dogs.[23] Indeed, because wolves are 'phylogenetically older' (i.e., older in terms of their genealogical history) and unlike us 'superbly equipped for hunting', some argue that humans initially survived on their leftovers.[24] Their collaborative hunting skills demonstrate profound differences in communication patterns as well: whereas dogs communicate primarily through scent, gesture and, in the case of pack hounds, vocalization, wolves use mostly visual cues to coordinate their stealth-hunting techniques. While all canids use some common facial expressions, body postures, tail-wagging patterns and vocalizations to communicate,[25] the profound behavioural differences of wolves make sustained cohabitation across species both rare and volatile.[26]

The most obvious behavioural differences perhaps lie in the various canid relationships with humans; dogs are tractable – they can be tamed and trained – but no other canids have ever proved so reliable.[27] The lifelong 'submission and obedience' to humans expected of dogs[28] have proved elusive in all attempts to domesticate *Canis lupus*. Perhaps best understood in terms of a profound 'xenophobia', most adult wolves resist assimilation to human ideals of social behaviour,[29] often turning on their would-be trainers with little or no warning.

Although pups across the species remain remarkably similar, the physical differences between adult wolves, who have produced the same general body type across the millennia, and dogs, in whom we see the broadest range of body types of all animals, further suggest that these two species adapted to different niches. Dogs who choose their own reproductive partners present the strongest challenge to the hypothesis of non-dog origins, which predicts that dog-selected breeding would create 'throwback' descendants who would increasingly resemble the original species. In other words, if they were directly descended from wolves, with each generation feral dogs breeding with each other should look increasingly more like them. Instead, such dogs progressively approximate a specific dog type, the medium-sized, reddish-brown appearance of the dingo.[30] Just like the

Pl. XII. Le Chien Turc et Gredin. T. 23 P. 219.

GRAND CHIEN LOUP

The 'Chien Turc et Gredin' and the 'Grand Chien Loup', from the Paris edition of Buffon's *Histoire naturelle* (1799–1805).

fossil and genetic evidence of early dogs, the bodies and behaviour of contemporary dogs both clarify some of the interconnections and highlight complications involved in defining dogs in relation to presumed progenitors in other species.

The special role of dogs as midwives to the birth of human civilization is complicated by the presence of wolves. For example, the copy (not the form) differs in breed dog and wolf 'collectibles', where the wild or savage wolf exhibits filial 'loyalty' to her own kind while the dog no less reliably pledges allegiance to the human. But the sticky questions of whether and how dogs (and humans) learn to extend these cultural values across species lines are overshadowed by the idea that

An advertisement for a decorative wall-plaque in the *Maine Sunday Telegram* (2 March 2003).

dogs are 'naturally' wolves. Humans, so this story goes, remove dogs from their natural state and transform (as they elevate) them to the world of culture, thereby exercising absolute dominion over the animal world. Once the weak wolf is converted to a dog by the civilizing association with humans, the other wolves in contrast become noble savages, dying off with what remains of their dignity in the stereotypic colonial role proscribed for indigenous peoples. The assumption here is that it is a manifest human destiny to dominate, and all others must perversely follow or naturally perish. Although any 'wild' animal could serve as the object of this Adamic power, at once

'Drifted in', from Josephine Diebitsch Peary's *My Arctic Journal* (1893).

naming and bringing the dog under human control, the crucial element in such a theory is the (re)creation of the dog as a dependent; re-made as servant or parasite, the dog is thus cursed for perverting nature.[31] These ideas may account for the current beleaguered status of dogs, but they all too conveniently excuse human abuse of them. At the very least, the use of these relationships as a natural justification for disparaging sentiments – such as the science writer Stephen Budiansky's controversial characterization of dogs as 'social parasites'[32] that have found an ecological niche in human tolerance – distorts our complicated cross-species history.

Many dogs do depend on humans, whether they simply feed from our refuse or more directly live as pets or working animals. Inhabiting a world largely structured by humans, however, involves creativity, intelligence and generosity on the part of the dog as well. While training methods require that humans take responsibility for dogs' dependance, they also assume a give-and-take in lieu of simply exercising 'natural' intimidation. This applies both to the 'military-style' methods popularized by William Koehler, which use physical 'corrections' in an aesthetic of absolute obedience, and to the 'clicker training' or positive-reinforcement methods touted by Susan Garrett, whose pamphlet of 2002, *Ruff Love*, signals an emerging aesthetic akin to the personnel management strategies fashionable today in corporate America.[33] When any of these training methods succeeds, dogs seek and find the guidance of reliable human leaders in avoiding trouble, especially common urban hazards such as aggressive dogs, cars and non-doggy people.[34] Maintaining even the ideal 'alpha dog status' involves telling dogs that humans are in charge in their own language.[35] Moreover, the extensive time and practice required by all these methods indicate that these relationships are made, not innate. From this perspective, domination begins to look like a highly cultured activity: assimilation to 'dog' as a culture (or set of cultures) shaped by shared languages.

While the interplay of dog training methods and human political systems provides a fascinating subject for cultural critique, even a refusal to train dogs illuminates assumptions about not only wolf 'nature' but also human political 'culture'. The anthropologist Elizabeth Marshall Thomas, one of the harshest critics of dogs being 'excessively brainwashed by human training',[36] wrote of her disappointment when she found that her pet dogs, left to train each other and to roam the city streets in defiance of leash laws, stay (interested in) dogs. 'The more I thought about it', she wrote, 'the more the ancient landed gentry of Europe came to seem like wolves, with one pair, the dominant male and female, owning a territory and the castles upon it and hunting the deer for miles around'.[37] It was needless for her to add that even her free-ranging dogs had fallen from this Edenic state. The widespread popularity of this kind of origin story and its long-standing relationship with racist and xenophobic ideologies of the human – exemplified more recently by the constant, almost compulsive connection of Adolf Hitler's codename 'Wolf' with his passion for dogs – bear further examination, particularly in the ways that this theory creates more problems than it resolves for the task of defining dogs.

These ideas of dog origins not only have a long history but also a long-standing interrelationship with racial hierarchies. Ancient Greek depictions of the peoples of India, for instance, develop their metaphoric association with dogs to present them as 'Europe's original noble savages'.[38] And more direct relationships with dogs as companion animals have influenced similarly disparaging views of one by another human culture. The ongoing and inordinate fascination of early Euro-American

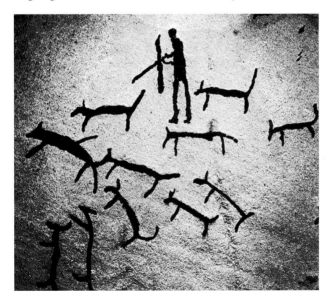

A cave painting of a Bronze Age hunter with (or of?) dogs.

explorers and later anthropologists with the indigenous women of South America, the Pacific Islands and Australia who feed puppies (and sometimes other mammals) from their own breasts becomes more understandable as part of this pattern of denigrating while exoticizing other people's lives with animals. Connected to the broader development of scientific species and racial taxonomies during the eighteenth century, this fascination also indicates how dogs played a decisive role in the incorporation of non-European 'animal practices' – the human–animal interactions through which human groups define (and often discriminate against) each other[39] – in the social invention of biology. However, the study of animal practices also shows that hunter-gatherer and subsistence agricultural peoples across the world consistently keep dogs as pets; much more than 'a pointless modern extravagance',[40] non-utilitarian relationships with dogs serve not only as a common source of discrimination but more importantly as a point of connection among peoples.

For good reasons, then, a conflict of origins characterizes the different myths of the cultural work of dogs. Ancient sculptures and carvings of dogs as far apart as Alaska, Greece, Peru and Persia indicate complex relationships between the mythic roles of dogs as human progenitors and protectors and the real roles of dogs specific to these societies. Just as actual dogs mediate human relationships with wild species such as wolves, their totemic representations often serve as a conceptual link between human worlds and those of other species. In this way, the significance of dogs within social systems led to special roles in philosophy, religion and medicine across the relatively self-contained histories of dogs in the Far East, Europe, Africa and the Americas through the early modern period, even before these belief systems began to inform each other. Beliefs about dogs underscore certain social practices or prohibitions, but these uses (even studied avoidance) of dogs relate to ancient traditions. Practical motivations thus become hard to separate from cultural values. The tremendous biological success of dogs may indeed hinge on their ability to get humans involved in raising their pups, but a narrow focus on this aspect of human–dog relationships also appeals directly to a bias toward the human viewpoint. Comparative documentation of human–dog relationships across cultures shows them to have been more often symbiotic than parasitic and offers a more comprehensive account than the dominance theories.

Dogs may depend on humans today, but many cultures demonstrate that there are significant advantages for human subsistence in living with dogs. In return for human assistance with caring for young and gathering food, dogs in many ways enhance basic human survival. Particularly through hunting literature, much attention has been devoted to how dogs help to feed humans, but the long history of dogs as a common source of clothing is less widely known. Along with jewellery, furniture and houses, clothes made expressly for dogs have been a popular symptom of 'excess' since the late nineteenth century,[41] and dogs commonly appear in fashion magazines as models for human as well as canine clothing. Urbanites accustomed to seeing pet dogs dressed in plastic rainwear and acrylic sweaters may see a recent book like *Knitting with Dog Hair* as the height of bourgeois absurdity,[42] but the practice of using dog hair in textiles is traditional among the Zuni and Coastal Salish tribes of North America, who kept dogs specifically for shearing,[43] as well as the European Arctic Samoyed people. The use of dog materials in clothing was also common in Europe into the nineteenth century; the *Encyclopædia Britannica* of 1810 notes that dog skins were used in making muffs, ladies' gloves, the linings

An Inuit dog sledge, from Robert E. Peary's *Snowland Folk* (1904).

of masks and 'a kind of buskin for persons in the gout'. In France especially, dog fur was imported in 'large quantities' and 'worked up in the black list of a particular kind of woollen cloth'.[44] At the end of the nineteenth century, an American Arctic explorer noted that 'dogskin trousers' were 'as warm as those made of bearskin but not so stylish'[45] and therefore typical winter garb among the peoples of the North, who like others across the Northern Hemisphere also depended on their dogs for hauling.

In the twenty-first century, turnspits powered by dogs and dog carts (the kind pulled by dogs, not ponies) have become rare antiques, and even dog sleds, though still used recreationally and in extreme contests like the Iditarod, have fallen by the wayside. Although mushing (dog sledding) as a sport remains plagued with allegations of cruelty,[46] it is also a testament to dogs' former status as favoured hauling animals, preferred especially in forbidding Arctic climates, where meat to feed them could be gathered along the journey. Speed was a factor as well: over distances of 16 kilometres (10 miles), sled dogs are the fastest land animals.[47] Taken together, these practices indicate how the ready availability of dogs leads to our variable definitions of them as easy sources of fur and skin, as well as food, rubbish disposal, rodent control, transportation and even alarm systems.

Eating dog is perhaps the most controversial animal practice today, because of the tremendous range of feelings stirred even by representations of dogs in Western industrialized cultures. Part of the reason is that dogs defy conventional standards about what counts as food – greedily consuming the carrion, rubbish, excrement and poison reviled by other animals – as well as how to eat, often begging for (even stealing), drooling over and dragging about their food.[48] But these different attitudes also signal profound cultural differences. For people all over the world, historically dogs serve as food containers or converters, consuming excess food during rich months and themselves becoming food sources for humans in lean ones. For their role in this unequal exchange of energy resources, in many cultures dogs have become sacrificial objects and religious symbols. Dogs are still eaten as a continuing part of ancient rituals among, for instance, the tribal peoples of North America, such as the Oglala Sioux, and historically seafaring peoples of the Far East, such as Filipinos.

The Oglala dog-meat traditions provide an especially interesting example of how dog cults and dog eating develop within a single culture. Until it became defunct early in the twentieth century, an Oglala fraternal society called the Dogs distinguished themselves through valour in war and horse stealing, taking names that described characteristic dog behaviours, and enforcing a strict taboo on their members against eating dog. Among all the other Oglala, however, dogs are traditionally raised not only to be pets but also to be consumed as part of major rituals, where dog stew is viewed not as meat but medicine. Sacrificial dogs are designated livestock through their upbringing, and they are slaughtered by a medicine man with the help of two female assistants, who anoint the dog and carefully position it so that its spirit will join the Thunder People who rule over life and death. In contrast, pet dogs are named and never become meat. Because the practice of eating dogs is so alien to the white American culture that surrounds and almost destroyed them, the Oglala today embrace these rituals as acts of cultural differentiation and recovery.[49] The demise of the dog cult along with the diminished scale of the dog-eating rituals, both direct results of the North American Indian genocide, inadvertently encourages white culture's tolerance of this otherwise taboo practice.

In contrast, ritual dog eating among tribal peoples of the Philippines – including Igorots (or Cordillerans), Ilocanos, Pampangueños and Pangasinenses – has become one of the few legal ways left of enjoying a traditional food. Widespread across the archipelago and traditionally a means of sustenance at sea, eating dog suddenly became restricted to religious, tribal or ethnic rituals with the passage of the country's first animal welfare act in 1998. This law has proved difficult to enforce because, as the film *Azucena* (Dog Meat) of 2000 shows, it is so common in the Philippines, associated especially with drinking men, like 'beer and nuts' in the USA.[50] Some traditional methods of slaughter, such as beating the animal to death, put this practice further at variance not only with Western sentiments but also with Filipinos themselves. For instance, an Igorot rite, rarely practised but protected by this new law, calls for butchering a dog who must be the pet of a family member; such rarefied traditions have little relation to the ongoing, massive and illicit trade in commercial dog meat.[51] A rare study of attitudes among Filipinos living in the US, part of an immigrant community numbering nearly 1,000,000 in California alone, shows how they come to internalize this deep ambivalence; sympathetic to the economic needs of poor people to consume cheap meat, even to sell pets for this purpose, the women surveyed also acknowledged that these practices were used as the basis of racial as well as ethnic discrimination against expatriate people from the Philippines.[52] For this group, conflicted cultural definitions of pets and meat make dog eating no simple matter of maintaining cultural ties.

Clearly, people in different cultures consume dogs ceremonially for many reasons, which include but are not limited to increasing their own valour in war, curing diseases of the spirit and honouring visitors. Even when they are not eaten, dogs serve as 'sacrificial lambs', so to speak, for the Bhotiyas in the Himalayas and the people of Ulawa in the Solomon Islands; for both groups, the death of the chosen dog is believed to take away the sickness and misfortunes of the people.[53] Many traditions connect dog eating with health still more directly. Now a euphemism in English for drinking more alcohol to cure a hangover, the actual 'hair of the dog that bit you' is an old European folk remedy believed to help heal dog bites, just as tricking dogs into eating some of one's own hair is said to transfer one's illness to the dog.[54] Along with dog hair and excrement, dog meat has long been used as medicine for physical ailments. The Oglala use dog meat to treat 'Indian sickness' (a generic term for all illnesses believed to carry over from pre-contact times),[55] and this medicinal approach was reported among ancient Greeks by Pliny the Elder and among medieval Muslims by al-Qazwini (the latter is all the more surprising because Islam prohibits eating dog).[56] In these practices, people are healed generally at the expense of the sacrificial dog, but in no case is the process perceived as a simple exchange of a dog's life for that of a human.

People who categorically oppose the practice of eating dog often ignore such complex cultural motivations, and in their ignorance assume that its continuation is fuelled only by cruelty and decadence. However, as the controversy surrounding the Filipino dog-meat trade suggests, the non-ceremonial practices common in modern urban settings throughout the world pose different problems. Likened by exotic food critics to lamb or mutton, dog meat has ancient and medieval histories as a secular delicacy and, in addition to the Philippines, it is served as such today in Korea, Nigeria and Spain.[57]

Such exoticizing, in turn, leads to nativist backlash in the form of laws that prohibit eating dogs, a prominent vehicle for anti-immigrant and especially anti-Asian sentiment in the US.[58] In a country in which some of the millions of euthanized dogs each year are now rendered and incorporated in packaged dog food,[59] it is difficult not to read the virulence of the cultural prohibition on dog eating as fuelled in part by repression of these gruesome and epidemiologically dangerous relationships created among contemporary pet dogs. Just as frankfurters or 'hot dogs', the quintessentially American food, have become a primary means of disposing of meat by-products, dog food has become an industrial destination of otherwise unwanted dog meat, legally allowed to be listed on packages under the innocuous-sounding ingredient names 'meat meal' and 'meat and bone meal'.[60] But it is not simply in defence of the wholesomeness of such dubious-sounding commercial products as Meato® and Gaines-burgers® – unrecoverable already for anyone who has read Ann Hodgman's notorious first-hand account of taste-testing such popular brands of dog food[61] – that people rush to condemn others who eat dog.

A cartoon of c. 1906: 'I Wonder Which was Father?'

A still from a Meato Dog Food television advertisement, c. 1960.

The use of dog eating as the basis for discriminating against others is itself an ancient tradition. Between neighbouring groups in the Americas, 'dog-eater' was often used as a common term of derision, whether applied by the Inca to the Huanca or the Shoshone to the Arapaho.[62] Just as dog eating has been encouraged among some, human abhorrence of the practice has been reinforced for thousands of years by other traditions, especially in the mythological accounts of conquering tribes. In Hindu mythology, the terms *Śvapacas* or *Śvapākas* – which can mean 'Dog-Cookers', 'Dog-Milkers' or even 'Dog-People' –

Dogs killed and processed in an animal market in Guangzhou.

range alongside tribal or ethnic names designating the categories of outcastes. Significantly, these cynomorphizing terms (terms that ascribe the characteristics of dogs to humans) are among the few words to gain general usage as a term for outcastes across India.[63] For Hindus, eating dogs thus becomes understandable only as an absolute limit within a larger context of human–animal identification; in this sense, the dog is to the cow what the outcaste is to the Brahmin. In story after story in the ancient Vedic scriptures, the (Brahmin) human must be continually separated from and elevated above the (outcaste) dog-people by maintaining certain relations and shunning others in this ongoing re-enactment of the history of tribal conquest.

In ancient history as well as myth, dogs are also regularly used as more literal points of reference to describe members of other cultures. In his study of myths of 'cynephali' or dog–man hybrids, the historian David Gordon White traces a pattern among ancient European, Indian and Chinese cultures of using these figures also to represent outcaste and far-flung peoples. Usually depicted with dog heads or faces, such people often display other dog-like traits, such as barking and tails. They exhibit more recognizably human behaviours (such as cannibalism and sodomy) and qualities (such as black skin and excessive body hair) only when these aspects represent the obverse of the ideals of the culture defining them as monsters. Dehumanized by their doglike ways, dog-men are perhaps most threatening in the ways in which they prove all too human. As Aesop's *Fables* illustrate, the reverse is true as well: in ancient Greece *kuwv* (dog) gained metaphorical meanings that included various human vices, including cowardice, immodesty and arrogance, suggesting that dogs in turn are debased by their undesirable human-like ways.[64]

A Byzantine 'dog-headed' St. Christopher.

As the ceremonial practices of dog eating suggest, however, other equally ancient mythological traditions invert this notion so that dogs clearly come before humans. Different peoples from nearly every continent trace their ancestry back to dogs. Across the Americas alone, various tribal origin stories depict dogs as primal parents, even crossing species lines as dog-wives (among Arawak, Dogrib, Chipewyan and Ojibwa tribes) and dog-husbands (Quinault, Tlingit, Haida, Nootka) to human progenitors. Mythical dogs act parentally as well, protecting the ancestors from wolves (Cherokee, Penobscot), people (Cheyenne, Potawatomi) and even witches (Micmac). More broadly, tribal peoples from Turkey to Mongolia also trace their descent from dogs; at one time surrounded by such groups, the ancient Han

Dog with relief decoration. Chinese tomb figure, Eastern Han dynasty, 2nd century AD, glazed pottery.

(with whom most contemporary Chinese people identify) understandably considered themselves the only humans in a world of Dog People.[65] The tales of the dingo among Australian Aborigines best represent the complexity of these theories, mixing accounts of the historic arrival of these dogs as companions / foodstuffs of Indonesian 'sea gypsies'[66] with the more suggestive Dreamings (a collective term for the historic time, actors, creative acts and cross-species relationships of their myths) of dingoes as both human ancestors and closest contemporaries.[67] Although varying widely in their accounts of primal human–dog relationships, these stories support the archaeological evidence that canine companionship has been pivotal to the development of human cultures. In this cross-cultural context, 'dog' seems much more than 'god' spelt backwards.

Mythical dogs also serve as markers of thresholds, especially those that lead to forbidden territories, in many ancient tales. Records of Australian Aboriginal Dreamings posit the dingo as

An Egyptian
bronze Anubis
with a moveable
jaw.

A carved Aztec
dog.

the origin of death. For ancient Egyptians, the rising of Sirius,
the dog-star and the brightest during the Nile's flood season,
signalled a new planting cycle along with the transition between
the worlds of the living and the dead. Fittingly for them, the
guide to the latter was the jackal- or dog-headed Anubis, god of
the dead. Similarly in Mexico, both Aztec and Maya belief systems valued dogs as guides for their masters, especially across
water in the underworld. Depictions of the god Xolotl (one of
many associated with the underworld) with a dog's head along
with actual dog skeletons carefully interred in tombs and at bodies of water, and more general canine associations with the
North and the underworld, all echo the Egyptian associations.[68]

Hellenistic legend also links the dog to cultural crossroads,
through association not only with Egypt, where Anubis was

worshipped in the city that the Greeks called Cynopolis, but also with war gods. While the Greeks abhorred their Ares and the Romans embraced their Mars, they alike kept dogs as pets as well as for utilitarian purposes, yet none of their own cities worshipped or even claimed the war god and his special animal as their own.[69] Instead, the dog's transitional role is reinforced in the most prominent mythical dog in Hellenistic cultures, the three-headed, dragon-tailed dog Cerberus, who guards the gate to the underworld. Although fearsome enough to have been the subject of Hercules' last and most difficult labour, Cerberus is also gullible, easily tricked by Psyche, the Sibyl of Cumae (who led Aeneas to the underworld), and, more recently, Harry Potter and friends. The powerful mythic associations are thus mitigated by the familiarity of dogs themselves.

Mutations across traditions tend to distil or streamline these associations. Hermanubis, a later Hellenistic fusion of dog associations, underscores their mediating role by identifying dogs more conventionally with Mercury or Hermes, the ever-present messenger god who both protects traders and guides the dead to their last home. In various Chinese myths, dogs both guide

Greek Kylix fragment (dog scratching) in the manner of the Euergides Painter, *c.* 500 BC, red-figure ceramic.

41

the dead like Anubis and guard the palace of heaven[70] like Cerberus. Linked in southern Chinese traditions to the return of food after a legendary flood and in northern ones to burial sacrifices, the Chinese Hound of Heaven echoes Hermanubis as a melding of regional myths.[71] And the power of such fusions persists through world religions today. In the Koran, the legendary Kitmir, a dog who guards seven young people fleeing persecution while they sleep in a cave ('the cave of the seven sleepers') for 309 years, is the only animal allowed to enter paradise. Echoing apocryphal Christian stories, this legend is interpreted by many as representing the resurrection of the dead and thus again positions the dog at the gateway of life and death.[72]

The roles of dogs as psychopomps, powerful imaginary figures for reckoning with the afterlife, reflect as well as reinforce profoundly ambivalent attitudes toward living dogs. The celebrated hunting skills of actual dogs as well as their notorious penchant for carrion may be the biological source of these gods, accounting for why such similar traditions exist among ancient Indian, Germanic, Armenian, Celtic, Iranian and Native American (including Iroquois, Huron, Algonquin and Menomeni) cultures. But their alignment with these mythical dogs often proves a mixed blessing for actual dogs. As the Oglala dog-eating ritual shows, in exchange for this power over the human imaginary, dogs are often used as sacrificial objects.

Some evidence suggests that the mutation of dogs into psychopomps also reflects the new pressures on human–dog relationships in increasingly urban environments. The abundance of dog representations from the late archaic through Hellenistic times include funereal monuments depicting dogs protecting their masters from mortal and otherworldly threats; such images suggest not only the traditional role of dogs as threshold creatures but also their increasing familiarity as

Cave canem ('Beware of the dog') on a Roman mosaic from Pompeii. As in many cultures today, this slogan typically flagged doorways and entrances.

companion animals.[73] Writing a primal relation in the stars, the Greeks saw Orion, the great celestial hunter, as followed by his two hounds, Sirius (the Greater Dog-star) and Procyon (the Lesser Dog-star, also known as Maera or Laelaps),[74] in a subsistence relationship that was becoming even for them increasingly rarefied. The identification of the star Sirius (a harbinger of spring) with dogs, death and the hot months or 'dog days of summer' in cultures across the northern hemisphere suggests further that attendant dog sacrifices are meant among other things to ensure a profitable agricultural cycle, the lifestyle that from neolithic times freed people from dependence on hunting.

The institutionalization of dog sacrifices in ancient city-states also shows how traditions of dog slaughter came to serve specifically urban public-health purposes. For instance, during the 'dog days' or hot months of summer, when rabies epidemics might be expected to peak, dogs were massacred in ancient Greek and ritually dismembered in ancient Chinese cities as part of ceremonies to ward off pestilence.[75] The dog gods were left out of these rituals, a coincidence that further connects these ancient belief systems to modern religious approaches to dogs. For instance, the Prophet Mohammed decreed a one-off extermination of rabid urban stray dogs that was used to justify such slaughters hundreds of years later in fourteenth-century Damascus, when the pathology of rabies was much better understood.[76] Mohammed's better-documented compassion for dogs and other animals as divine creations fell by the wayside, another example of how ancient egalitarian ideas about dogs and people were eclipsed by more contemporary interests in hierarchical relationships. These associations had become so entrenched by the early twentieth century that a rabid dog served as a mechanism for destroying the one equitable sexual relationship experienced by Janie, the African-American heroine of Zora Neale Hurston's *Their Eyes Were Watching God* (1937). Rabid dogs do not simply symbolize oppression but more literally become an excuse for the entrenchment of authoritarian social structures.

More clearly, the pivotal roles of dogs at the crux of the classic epics of India and Greece assert the primary cultural importance of dog–human relationships. The widely influential ancient Indian epic *Mahābhārata* ends with a story of redemption through a faithful dog whom the hero is pressured to abandon yet elects to retain, risking all the celestial rewards he has earned for a journey through which he loses everything else. Fortunately the dog, whose 'loyalty, devotion and especially love' proves more worthy to the hero than eternal rewards, 'reveals himself to be none other than the God of Righteousness',[77] so the implicit point that dogs are better than gods

The Virgin Mary feeding a dog, an illustration in *The Miracles of the Blessed Virgin Mary*, from Gondar, Ethiopia, c. 1670–80.

remains moot. What is more curious is that the human's faithfulness is elaborately interrogated while the dog's (after all, supernatural) loyalty goes unquestioned in a poem that remains a mainstay of the popular shadow puppet theatre in predominantly Muslim Indonesia.

Working 500 years earlier in ancient Greece and also probably condensing older tales, Homer in his comparably influential epic poem *The Odyssey* gives an equally important if more literal canine character a pivotal role at the end. Punctuating the account of the hero Odysseus' travels are several brief mentions

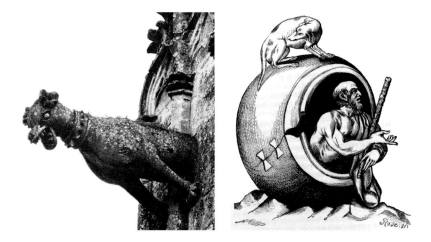

of his dog Argus, pining away for his master. When the disguised hero finally returns home, the dog is the only one who recognizes him and, at this final reunion, the long-suffering dog immediately dies. Greek philosophers saw this dog as instructive. In this act of recognition, Argus was said to illustrate Socrates' idea of the dog as the 'true philosopher', who unlike the human characters passes the test of knowledge and ignorance by seeing through his master's disguise and welcoming his return. But Socrates' magnanimous interpretation of Argus contrasts with that of Diogenes and the Cynics, for whom the philosophic dog should withhold his favours until the master produces gifts,[78] which of course Odysseus never does. Advocates of this philosophic dog cult rejected the fictional Argus, who himself offers the gift of love and becomes the only mortal to provoke the otherwise unremorseful hero to tears. Again, the dog provides the hero's ultimate test of character, proving more faithful and tenacious than human companions.

Whereas the sympathetic dog conducts the penultimate test in the Indian and Greek epics, an encounter with a very different kind of dog tests the northern European Irish Celtic hero Cú Chulainn in the Ulster sagas of AD 300–400. Later Celtic myths describe hunts involving thousands of incredibly skilled hounds, indicating that the ancient Irish revered human–dog working relationships. But the Cú Chulainn myth also develops the dog's symbolically conflicted values as guardian and adversary. According to this legend, Culann, a renowned smith, kept the fiercest dog in the land until he inadvertently set it on his young nephew. In self-defence, the boy killed the dog but offered himself as a replacement for so valuable an animal. A druid renamed the boy Cú Chulainn, literally 'the Hound of Culann',[79] and this moniker grew to mean the Hound of Ulster, signalling how the fearless boy 'who willingly exchanges a long life for a brief and glorious one'[80] grows from social liability to the supreme warrior of the Ulster army. For the Irish, comparison with the loyalty and fierceness of dogs in this pre-Christian culture remains complimentary, indicating the high value of dogs as well as their danger.

In all of these tales, a critical moment in his relationship with a dog secures the hero's final transformation between lives, whether mortal and immortal or nomadic and settled. This shows how increasingly literal representations of dogs retain the more ancient associations of mythical dogs with guarding or gate-keeping (roles themselves influenced by the ancient and actual work of livestock-guarding dogs). The dogs of these texts, which have become central to Eastern and Western literary canons respectively, do not stand in for humans so much as they enable the human hero to become (or to reveal himself as) more than he can be when among only humans. What these dogs dramatize spectacularly is a reversal of the dog–man

projections; instead of denigrating him by association, the hero's relationship with a dog helps him to internalize – and thereby accept responsibility for negotiating – the borderlands defining human identity and society.

As the various associations with death suggest, however, this ambivalence can be a liability, particularly when dogs are cast in roles that represent the most repellent aspects of communal living. In ancient Indian, Native American and Near Eastern traditions, dogs become symbols of abhorrent behaviour, and contact with them renders believers, their belongings and even places (especially places of worship) unclean. Consequently, in Arabic *kelb* (dog) is a pejorative term that becomes insulting when applied to humans,[81] and notable exceptions – such as Kitmir, the lone dog in paradise – only prove this rule.[82] Interestingly, 'dog' becomes an epithet usually reserved for non-believers in Muslim as well as Christian and Jewish religious texts, showing how in their estimations of each other these groups continue to rely on dogs as a point of reference to draw and re-draw boundaries.

More subtly and constantly, words for dogs trace distinct lines of interaction and conflict within and across cultures. The central Asian geographical crossroads of many traditions, corresponding with the most recent genetic evidence of the locus of human settlement and dog origin, have inspired much philological speculation. While words for dog (like the Sanskrit *śvan* and Greek *kuōn*) are directly related in the common Indo-European linguistic traditions, debates about their structural similarities to the Mandarin Chinese term *ch'üan* imply a more universal role for dogs in defining cultures.[83] As with the dog-gods, however, pinpointing the connections between biological origins and their representations proves elusive. Still, some curious patterns persist.

If the wide range of material properties and social uses of dogs have made defining them difficult, then it can be no surprise that the words we use for them have become increasingly complex over the millennia as well. For instance, in modern Japanese the *kanji* (Chinese characters or ideograms) for *inu* (dog) combines with others to signal derogatory compound terms for humans like 'loser' and the even more culturally specific pejorative, 'cowardly samurai'. Stylized as a character radical,[84] it becomes part of the structure of the *kanji* for 'crime', 'barbarian' and 'madness'. In a combination term like 'rabies' (the characters of which can be translated literally as 'mad dog sickness'), it figures as both character and radical, reinforcing the long-standing association of dogs with a disease deadly to (and spread by) humans and other animals. Although the etymology of character radicals is speculative at best, the consistency with which this one is included in the terms for other species native to the region – including wolf and golden eagle (as a character) and fox, wolf, wild boar, monkey and otter (as a radical) – suggests that the familiarity of dogs makes them useful for understanding other animals as well as humans. Such linguistic evidence of the dog as a primary point of reference is more pronounced in the Oglala Sioux language, where *šunka* (dog), integrated into *šunkawakan* (horse), reflects an initial perception of these equine European transplants as a sacred kind of dog.[85] Representing dogs thus appears significant to the development of language and its interrelationships with growing understanding of complex natural and cultural phenomena.

In English this process is also illustrated by etymological studies of the word 'dog'. Unlike the word 'hound', which has common roots across Indo-European, Semitic and central Asian languages, the origins of the word 'dog' are less well known, stemming from an Anglo-Saxon verb that means to guard.[86] Standing in contemporary English for not just the most familiar canids but also worthless men, fun fellows (hence the current hiphop version, 'dawg', meaning home-boy or dude), ugly women, other animal species ('prairie dogs'), males of other animal species ('dog foxes' as distinct from 'vixens'), even andirons, dog is an 'eminently metaphorical' term.[87]

But the developments of these meanings can also reflect specific social developments. In a classic structuralist study of words, William Empson focuses on the development of the English uses of 'dog' between the sixteenth and eighteenth centuries. Through familiar literary examples, ranging from William Shakespeare to Samuel Johnson, this analysis shows how the increasing use of 'dog' to describe men makes class structures seem less rigid in their 'hearty' uses, such as 'sea dog' for the otherwise abject sailor. Yet these human 'dog' terms also serve as a defence against social revolution in their 'patronizing' applications, such as 'gay young dog' for the errant aristocrat.[88] Such terms reflect the contested rise of rationalist and humanist sentiments towards other humans and animals during the period, a new philosophical emphasis on feelings that led to radical interrogations of medieval Christian hierarchies of being, which arguably ushered in the Enlightenment era. From interpersonal to literary applications, the uses of 'dog' reflect

LATINE Canis. **ITALICE** Cane.
GALLICE Chien. **GERMAN.** Hund.

The margin note reads:

Dogs in a group, from Conrad Gesner's *Historiae animalium* (Zürich, 1560).

SEQVVNTVR *tria canum genera, quæ Hector Boëthius Scotis peculiaria eſſe ſcribit: ſed ut Io. Caius Anglus nos monuit, non minus frequentes in Anglia ſunt, Effigies eorum Heinricus à S. Claro Metropolitanæ Eccleſiæ Glaſguenſis in Scotia decanus, uir nobilitate & eruditione præclarus, per doctiſſimum uirum Io. Ferrerium Pedemontanum nobis tranſmiſit.*

CANIS Britannicus ſiue Scoticus alius, ſurũ deprehenſor, Scotis uocatus an̄ **Sluth bownd.** Conferatur hic cum Anglorum **Bluthund** eid eſt, Cane ſagace ſanguinario. Similem quidem huic Canem ſagacem ſanguinarium pictum Io. Caius mihi, cuius effigies mox ſequetur cum loro, ſed hoc & ſequente ſagacibus ſuum maiorem eſſe ſcribit. Canis hic inquit Hector Boëthius, haud maior eſt odoriſequis: ſed ut plurimum ruſſus, nigris inſperſus maculis, aut niger ruſſis. Tanta uero his ſagacitas ineſt, ut fures furtóq́ ablata perſequantur, & deprehenſos continuò inuadant. Quod ſi fur, quò fallat, fluuium traiecerit, quo loco fluuium ingreſſus eſt & ipſiſe præcipitant, & in aduerſam deuenientes ripam, in gyrum circunquaq́ præcurrere non ceſſant, donec odoratu ueſtigia aſſequti ſunt, &c. GERM. **Schlatthund/ Bluthund.**

an ongoing and pervasive pattern of using dogs to negotiate cultural changes.

In some cases, the cross-cultural mythological use of dogs specifically to signify people who are 'not us' suggests a universal human history not of understanding the world so much as of misunderstanding it. For instance, Christopher Columbus confused Cariba, the native name for the New World island on which he disembarked and the root of the term Caribbean, with 'cani-ba' or the 'canine' great Khan of Cathay, China, whose name in turn was confused with the Latin *canis* or dog.[89] While the famous Italian explorer's etymology certainly shows that he was willing himself closer to his desired destination in the Far East, it also draws together long-standing traditions of representing social difference – or, rather, misrepresenting differences among humans as cross-species differences. According to David Gordon White, Columbus's mistake is not exceptional but symptomatic for the dog-man, the ancient figure of human otherness that continued as a stock character in bestiaries throughout the late Middle Ages and subsequently gained new meanings (if not attributes) in early modern European depictions of New World peoples.

Even among users of the same language, dog terms enable discrimination and social power imbalances. In English, the association of 'dog' with maleness distinguishes males over females or 'bitches'. The consequences of these associations can be charted in modern times through the novelist E. B. White's recollection that, in the 'post-Victorian' suburban America of his childhood, the prejudice against keeping canine bitches ostensibly concerned class – 'One's washerwoman might keep a bitch, or one's lawn cutter, but not one's next-door neighbor' – but ultimately left him with the impression 'that there was something indecent and unclean about she-things in general'.[90]

'A Brazilian Cannibal', from *A Collection of Engravings, Etchings and Woodcuts of Various Sizes, Mainly Illustrating the Costumes of Different Nations...*, a folio compilation of c. 1550–1650 now in the British Library, London.

For this bourgeois boy, working-class people and dirty female animals became conceptually linked through the terms for (and practices concerning) bitches.

Such social prejudice against keeping bitches among people with the means, space and interests to do so proved a challenge for dog breeders,[91] who over the twentieth century were faced with a decreasing availability of intact female dogs. As White indicates, conceptual associations more than lived experiences create these conditions. Writing at the same time, the pioneering Austrian animal ethologist and one-time Nazi party member Konrad Lorenz has become notorious for the overlap in his theories of animal breed and species with his sordid and perhaps murderous eugenic work at the Office for Race Policy of the Third Reich.[92] Lorenz's comparatively progressive attitudes toward sex and gender that emerge in his writing about his pet dogs are thus all the more startling. These latter notions become particularly evident when he juxtaposes his own categorical preference for the canine bitch above all animals – based on 'the fineness of its perceptions and in its capacity to render true friendship' – with the observation: 'Strange that in English her name has become a term of abuse'.[93] The pronoun shift here is telling. While the Anglo-American prejudice against bitches struck the Austrian animal scientist as odd, Lorenz's own it / her fluctuation in turn suggests anxiety about the social consequences of this sentiment; preference for 'it' is only logical, but prejudice against 'her' is the unfortunate reality of the bitch's life.

Today these associations inform the reluctance of contemporary American owners to neuter male (but not female) dogs.[94] And the preferential treatment of males leads not only to the denigration of their female counterparts but also the various groups of people (in White's case, women and the working poor) associated with bitches. In this way, historic uses of dogs as imaginative vehicles for human prejudices seems only to have grown more pronounced during the twentieth century, when 'dog' in the English language gained the colloquial meaning 'ugly woman'.

The word 'bitch' in particular illustrates how these terms became political in the twentieth century, especially amid the rise of the new social movements of the 1960s and '70s. Writing during this period, Colette Audry notes that the French word *chienne* (bitch) is 'the label tagged on any woman, in films or novels, who dares to exploit her physical potential'.[95] Although dogs more generally represent what people revile in others, Audry argues, the bitch is a special imaginative target for moral condemnation of sexual behaviour. In refusing to use the conventional pet name *ma petite chienne* (my little bitch) for her own pet German shepherd, she sees herself as indicating, 'with great precision, the limitations of our relationship'.[96] In the 1960s Audry thus tried to avoid repeating what she saw as a broader social problem of controlling women through the term 'bitch', but this in turn limited her own relationship with her dog.

With the rapid development of feminist philosophy and politics, this approach (or avoidance) began to seem part of the problem rather than the solution. The sea change in attitudes became visible through women's reappropriation of 'bitch' as a term of human identity. Since 1996 the editors of the magazine *Bitch* (subtitled *Feminist Response to Pop Culture*) have embraced this term as their banner, provoking direct critical enquiry into these and other historically problematic yet continuing patterns of representing women. Redeployments of this term include women in hiphop culture calling themselves 'bee-atches' to reclaim the terms of their own identity both immediately from male 'dawgs' and more broadly to tell their own stories, following the call-and-response pattern of many poetic traditions. While these new meanings of 'bitch' aim to improve the living conditions of women more than those of dogs, together these developments show how words not only symbolize but also more importantly regulate relationships among people as well as dogs.

But these words also affect the relationships among dogs, albeit less obviously. Commenting as well on the rarity of urban bitches in post-war Britain, J. R. Ackerley speculates that their absence derives not only from the 'trouble' caused by their 'seasons' (heats) in cramped cityscapes, as people move from houses to flats, but also the kind of irrational fear and loathing that White recalls. These qualities converge in 'the outraged puritan mind prating of public decency and the corruption of the young', the person who follows a moral imperative cruelly to break up dogs copulating in the street, regardless of the high risk of fatal damage to the female.[97] For Ackerley, advocating sexual freedom for people and dogs alike, such a person merits deepest contempt. What is more, his example most clearly illustrates the social backlash for all of the metaphorical association of bitches with women, the transference onto dogs of the human male chauvinism or reactionary machismo that similarly limits and damages human lives.

The contexts of these twentieth-century examples – all cultural critiques that address the problems of 'bitches' – reflect the primacy of dogs in mediating nature, culture and the contested borderlands between these powerful if imaginary spaces, a recurrent theme in the chapters that follow. Growing acceptance of the idea of the dog as an interactive part of cultural structures can be seen through trends in dog training methods, which have become more sensitive to the dog's role in shaping social relations. But such approaches are no less burdened by the multiple and conflicted ideas about the beginnings and futures of these relationships that characterize the meshes of human and canine orders.

Taken together, archaeological, mythological and etymological evidence suggests profoundly mixed feelings about the origins and definitions of dogs, yet these in turn reflect a deeply shared experience. In addition to providing each other directly with sources of food and shelter, humans and dogs for thousands of years have mutually benefited from the complex relationships involved in hunting, guarding and herding other animals. Perhaps never simply utilitarian, the various forms of human–dog companionship have become only more conflicted in the past few centuries. As well as continuing today in traditional roles specific to nomadic and village life, humans and dogs are also creating new relationships specific to our increasingly industrial environments to take on such new challenges as mobility assistance, drug-sniffing and bomb-detecting.

The broad range of dogs' abilities may ensure adaptation to evolutionary niches over millennia, but through the past few centuries it has been not simply their physical adaptability that has ensured their prevalence within human-dominated environments. Their biological ability to subsist on our waste may account for their persistence through a period of mass extinction of other species by humans, but our shifting of the cultural values of dogs in terms of breed suggests more specific reasons why worldwide human population growth ensures theirs. The next chapter explores how this physical and social flexibility has enabled humans to forge not only utilitarian relationships but also something that for many proves even more profitable, the breed dog.

2 Breeds

'Breed' names may now be the most familiar terms with which people make sense of the broad range of possibilities among dogs, but, like 'species' ones, they have also become among the most contested. Contemporary dog breeders cite all sorts of cultural evidence – typically paintings and carvings, like those of the ancient Babylonians and Egyptians – to argue that the human invention of breeds dates back thousands of years. Some even claim that these images are proof that certain breeds are human-initiated hybrids, separately derived strains of different animals.[1] But even reading dog breeds into these images is difficult. Although the uniform canine shapes could suggest breeding programmes,[2] this aspect is also in keeping with the overall stylized patterns of representing humans and other animals in such images. Most importantly, this 'proof' of the ancient history of breeds appears so only with hindsight, after the creation of continuous pedigrees, closed stud books and breed standards within the past 300 years. Again, the idea of dogs as human creations proves more alluring than the evidence that the species history of dogs is much older and involves more complicated relationships with humans and other animals. Just as the origins of dogs are profoundly mixed, the impact of this relatively new way of seeing dogs has been both great and detrimental.

Near Eastern (Mesopotamian or Babylonian), Middle Bronze Age (2000–1800 BC) terracotta statuette of a dog.

Breed proponents argue compellingly that the creation or rather 'preservation' of dog breeds and their regulation through breed societies and dog shows have promoted popular interest in dogs. Moreover, their work in breed societies often includes helping to educate pet owners about how to care for their dogs.[3] Especially in recent years, these groups have also provided charitable services that promote the health, recovery and rescue of dogs, and even people. And they have fostered productive debates about reproductive responsibilities, from more immediate issues, such as spaying / neutering and finding homes for puppies, to long-term concerns, such as 'pure-bred' population genetics. Although temperament and performance evaluation has yet to be required of dogs entering the show ring,[4] breed recognition has led to growing awareness of the different psychological and

The pedigree back to 1782 for John A. Cowen's blue-and-tan 'Ask 'im II', pupped in 1874.

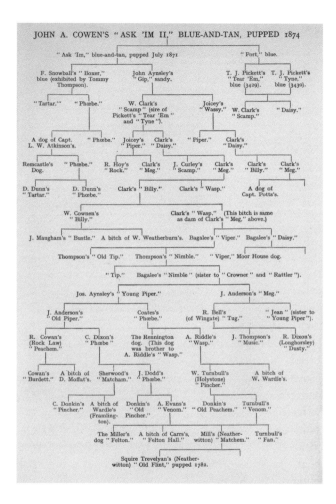

JOHN A. COWEN'S "ASK 'IM II," BLUE-AND-TAN, PUPPED 1874

physical needs of dogs. Ideally, knowledge of breed traits can even help people to make informed decisions when selecting canine companions, and this knowledge undoubtedly has been enriched through the dedication of fanciers to their preferred breed dogs.

Henri Toulouse-Lautrec, *Bouboule: Mme Palmyre's Dog*, 1897, pastel on board.

But breed has also been a major source of problems, in part because 'breed' (like 'dog') is hard to define. An authoritative consensus on especially breed-specific behaviour traits is rare, and even when achieved it poses problems because these systems derive from a definition based on visual standards. Although another important way of distinguishing dogs is by their behaviour – stereotypally, shepherd dogs herd, hounds hunt, retrievers retrieve, etc. – any dog can exhibit any degree of these traits, indicating how widespread they can be. More often, such descriptive terms are used to designate breed group-ings. For pet-dog owners, professional breeders and indeed anyone who comes in regular contact with dogs, these pure-bred character profiles encourage instantaneous (and perhaps misplaced) trust and fear based on what breed a dog resembles.[5]

To be fair, breed-club members have been among the most vocal in criticizing such profiles, for instance, in the nineteenth (and quickly recalled) edition of the American Kennel Club's 'canine bible', *The Complete Dog Book*, which included descriptions of several breeds as 'unsuitable for families with children'.[6] But their commitment to dog showing, which is often the breeders' primary objective and has become the chief means of regulating human interventions in dog breeding worldwide, exacerbates this problem of privileging appearance. Dog-show judges reward what a dog looks like and how it behaves in the show ring, not how it thinks, behaves or fares otherwise over the course of a lifetime. As long as the dog-show aesthetic remains overwhelmingly visual, people with the most hands-on experience but with no necessary training in behaviour or genetics will have the greatest impact on dogs' lives.[7]

Outside the show ring, the high public profile of these events not only encourages widespread breed recognition but also encourages fads for certain breeds, largely to the detriment of all dogs. A little knowledge in a loosely regulated market proves a dangerous thing for both dogs and humans, leading people with no other awareness of dogs to desire a Rottweiler because it 'looks tough' or to breed collies because Lassie re-runs guarantee high prices for the puppies. The phenomenon of 'puppy mills' – kennels producing breed dogs as stock for pet stores, situations that encourage egregious neglect and cruelty – attests to the industrial scale of breed-dog commercialization.

Even when born and bred in the best possible conditions, a breed dog is categorically the product of documented inbreeding, what breeders prefer to call 'line breeding'. A show-quality breed dog must descend exclusively from other breed members, all registered by recognized breed societies (in turn usually affiliated with national kennel clubs). Stemming from an

DOG SHOW.

abbreviated family tree, the breed dog usually carries genes that cause congenital physical disorders or defects partially caused by heredity – including cleft palate, haemophilia and progressive retinal atrophy leading to blindness.[8] Again, the genetic problems are compounded by the use of physical type as a standard of selecting show-quality dogs, who are the most likely to be bred. Through the complex arrangements of genes underpinning differences in outward appearance, what may seem superior physical qualities when judged in a show ring may be indelibly linked to disease. The associations of hip dysplasia among German shepherds with show breeders' preference for sloped backs may be one such instance.[9] In addition to these inherent risks of lifelong and progressive physical problems, some breed standards inspire 'cosmetic' or 'elective' surgical procedures such as tail docking and ear cropping, which although recently banned in many European countries are still commonplace in the usa and Canada.[10] However, for all of these problems, breed dogs gain social approbation that is withheld from their non-breed comrades (who will be the focus of the next chapter), and more broadly the concept of breed shapes canine and human lives.

For those of us who take special interest in the dogs around us, it is difficult to avoid seeing individual dogs as mixtures or exemplars of the various breeds. Although such evaluations

Omar Marcoux, *Dog Show*, 1937 ('folk art' piece from a rural arts exhibition held on the patio of the us Department of Agriculture building).

may seem benign when applied to random dogs encountered in the street, they can mean life or death, for instance, to dogs in animal shelters, who are far more likely to be adopted (and not destroyed) if they can be advertised as members of a desirable breed. Less obvious still are how, in applying current standards of breed to and against dogs, we humans make judgements about each other and ourselves. To make these assumptions plain involves approaching breed as a modern invention, not simply mirroring but more purposefully complementing the more familiar human categories of identity such as race, sex and species, which also gain new power through their scientific applications in Western industrial cultures. The allure of breed, the power of this illusion to overshadow our everyday experiences with dogs, appears more purposeful when these present conditions are situated amid wider historical developments.

This conflicted position of breed dogs today – the reason why, for instance, their health problems remain difficult if not impossible to resolve – stems from the peculiar and often intertwined histories of the breeds themselves. Against the species history of dogs, much of which has been lost over the millennia, canine breed histories look strikingly recent and recoverable. In the previous chapter, the different breeds illustrated the bewildering variety of dogs in terms of behaviour and physique, but it remains to be seen how and why the formation of these breeds has involved a combination of canine flexibility and human interventions more directly. One complication is the ancient use of the term 'breed' to mean a variety of categorizations, many of which lack the current associations with continuous pedigrees and physical standards.

Dogs have long been divided into groups, but these divisions are not legible as breeds in the conventional sense. The earliest

Li Di (967–1043 AD), *Hunting Dog*, album leaf, colours on silk.

taxonomy of dogs, included in the so-called Chinese *Book of Rites*, dates from 800 BC and offers only three vague categories: hunting, guarding and edible,[11] with no mention of pets.[12] Xenophon (the historian), writing 400 years later, lists early Greek dogs according to national affiliation but does not systematically link these 'breeds' to distinct physical characteristics.[13] By AD 945 the laws of a king of Wales, Hywel Dda (Hywel the Good), provided 'the first detailed classification of dogs in the world',[14] by correlating some physical and behavioural characteristics. However, the fact that the 'colwyn', itemized simply in these laws as a special category of non-working dog owned only by the nobility, has been interpreted variously as 'spaniel'[15] and 'lapdog'[16] indicates that Hywel Dda's taxonomy is too vague to designate even the breed groupings, let alone specific breeds, that organize kennel club records and events today. Across these texts the progressive movement toward establishing and embellishing hierarchies within the canine species is clear. But contemporary notions of breed proceed from more than simple descriptions of dogs and differentiating one from another.

Rather than attempt to catalogue the various breeds of dogs or compare their merits, in what follows I will outline how breed secures certain meanings for dogs in ways that both alter their roles within human society and reflect larger changes in human–dog relationships. For instance, in Europe and West Asia, hostility towards dogs as pets is intimately connected with both the rise of monotheistic traditions and the explosion of urban populations; consequently, theological changes that made Christianity more receptive to pet-keeping in the Middle Ages put the cultures associated with it at odds with those identified with more literal interpretations of Judaism and Islam.[17] As breed dogs became global commodities, by the end of the nineteenth century, these new approaches to old animal practices more broadly placed the dog at the centre of cultural conflicts, for example, concerning dogs as luxury pets or meat. In order to see how physiological and social differences among dogs and people alike came to be accounted for in terms of breeding (in the broadest sense), it is necessary to examine how historically this concept gained currency in mixed communities of humans, dogs and other species.

This canine breed system or, more precisely, the division of the bewildering array of the world's dogs into haphazardly sorted and named family groupings, emerged as part of the process by which the world's people were for the first time scientifically catalogued according to race, sex and gender. And this taxonomic process was inseparable from the imperialist politics it served. If culture and nature seemed difficult to separate in definitions of the dog, then they became all the more confounded in this recent history of sub-distinctions, such as breeds. Within this broader context, animal practices that seemed acceptable from the perspective of industrial affluence, for instance ending traditional working relationships such as hauling in the interest of animal welfare, can look from other perspectives like an imperial extension of fantasies of so-called Oriental peoples[18] through animal bodies similarly conceived of as exotic servants or sex slaves. Cross cultural representations of greyhounds and Fu or Fo dogs show how specific qualities have become attached to different kinds of dog, since these symbolic associations take shape and continue in representations of breed dogs today. More recently, with the invention of the breed dog through the dog show in Britain and its related social-regulatory institutions in the nineteenth century, the two traits have become fused, both socially acceptable and controlled in breed-dog bodies.

Symbolic values associated with dogs are as influential as behaviour and physical appearance in shaping modern breed aesthetics. As part of the European transition from feudal to imperial societies, two common canine associations – fidelity and lust – were secured through images and stories of certain types of what became breed dogs, respectively hounds and toy dogs. Through the development of royal hounds, especially greyhounds, fidelity became the provenance of the breed dog in a process that also dissociated this type from its more mixed Near Eastern history, where it had been a prized possession of both the Arab nobility and the nomadic peoples they displaced. The corresponding association of lust with the toy or lap dog, of which the dogs once prized by the Chinese as the Fu or Fo dog (literally, 'dog of Buddha') are emblematic, also shows how these conventional Western associations did not develop in a vacuum but rather in response to increasing

Sakai Hoitsu, *Western Dogs*, 1814, ink, gold and colour on wood.

contact with and awareness of various Eastern cultures (let alone the cultures of Africa, Australia and the Americas).

Images of canine faithfulness characterize Classical funereal iconography, and these idealized depictions in turn appear to have modelled the primary significance of dogs in early medieval Western religious painting. But the greyhound, one of the most readily recognizable types of dogs, secured this meaning as the centuries passed by, bringing together more precise associations with noble birth and canine fidelity.[19] In part, this was due to the long-standing approbation of this type of dog in the Middle East. In Arabic, the *saluki* or *salugi* (male hound or greyhound) is also referred to as *el hor* (the

noble one) as distinct from *kelb* (dog and, more generically, a term of derision). An indication of the complex range of meanings that dogs can have within and across cultures, these terms distinguish the greyhound-type canines that according to legend were brought by tribal peoples from western Asia to Europe and used specifically to hunt, and over time to compete in the sport of coursing outlined below. Ancient Greek, Roman and Persian manuscripts contain descriptions that not only closely resemble each other but also describe the sleek bodies and swift hunting skills associated with modern greyhounds. But the unequivocal association of this type of dog with both fidelity and nobility came much later, as illustrated by the disputed etymology of 'greyhound' in English.

This has been traced variously to the Dutch *grüss-hound* from *grypen* (to grip), the ancient British *grech* or *greg* (dog) and the Latin *gradus* (degree). The last is the source of the most popular theory, that the word greyhound is a corruption of the descriptive phrase 'great hound'. Although the second possibility seems most likely, the last is supported by the Danish Canute Laws (later the Forest Laws), enacted in England in 1016, which decreed: 'No mean person may keep any greyhounds'.[20] Once owning this kind of dog became a symbol of a person's social power, then it follows that a greyhound by association gained a similarly elevated social status over other dogs. In this instance, breed moves from a method of categorization to a means of ranking dogs, who in this process make human power relations visible. Tautologically, the greatest dog becomes the most loyal and the most loyal the greatest (because closest) to the human rulers.

The fusion of these breed associations is clarified in the medieval story of the holy greyhound St Guinefort, the dog of a French knight, whose martyrdom was documented and rejected by the Roman Catholic Church in the mid-thirteenth century. A Church inquisitor records the story of how the knight left the greyhound to guard his infant son. After a huge serpent had entered the room, a fierce battle ensued, in which the dog killed the snake, the baby fell out of the cradle and everyone got covered in blood. The knight returned and, mistaking his sleeping son for dead and Guinefort for the murderer, immediately killed his dog. After he had discovered the snake's remains, the knight then, according to the Inquisitor, 'deeply regretting having unjustly killed so useful a dog', threw the dog's corpse into the well, covered it with stones and planted trees to commemorate the event.

This barebones version of Guinefort's legend may seem over the top, yet in many ways it exceeds even the Inquisition account. Although the Church officially disavowed the holy greyhound, Guinefort was worshipped locally as a healing saint even into the nineteenth century.[21] Moreover, his story echoes a

King Harold of England out hawking with his hounds, scene from the Bayeux Tapestry.

tale often told of animal devotion and human ignorance. With different animals starring as martyr and menace, the story appears to have ancient sources, including the *Panchantra*, a 2,600-year-old Indian treatise on the education of princes, as well as more recent Greek, Latin, Arabic[22] and even Thai variants.[23] The more directly parallel Welsh legend of Llywelyn and his hound Gelert may be an antecedent, but representations of this dog too as a greyhound suggest more widespread cultural shifts towards seeing this particular kind of breed dog as an exemplar of dogged devotion.[24]

This approach to extreme canine fidelity as a breed member's birthright also appears in more recent commemorative accounts that focus on individual dogs. The Edinburgh monument to Greyfriars Bobby, the nineteenth-century dog who visited his Scottish master's grave every day for fourteen years, realistically depicts him as a Skye terrier. Similarly, the life-size sculpture of Hachiko, the twentieth-century akita who for nine years waited daily for his dead master's return at the Shibuya

Claude-Michel Clodion, a terra-cotta mausoleum for 'Ninette', c. 1780–85.

train station in Tokyo, reinforces the notion not merely of the dog's constancy but also draws a connection between this idealized personality trait and the breed dog's breeding. Reciprocally, honouring the faithful canine companion elevates the human; for instance, Mackworth Island, a popular park in my city, Portland, Maine, was donated by a former governor in honour of his red (or Irish) setter dogs buried there, but subse-

Sir John Soane's design for a canine residence, c. 1779.

72

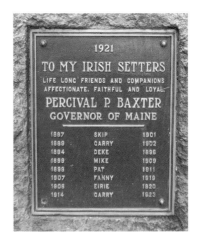

Monument to Percival P. Baxter's Irish setter dogs, Mackworth Island, Portland, Maine.

quently it augmented the man's reputation for philanthropy. Through Guinefort's story, canine loyalty may not exactly be rewarded, but it is definitely honoured in memory of the greyhound as protector and symbol of nobility.

As both a chivalric emblem and a favoured animal companion, the medieval greyhound – again long associated with 'greatness' – was ideally suited to this role in feudal culture. Reinforced for centuries to come by the constant presence of greyhounds in European representations of royalty, especially royal hunts, this particular kind of dog's connections with nobility and masculinity ensured that greyhounds were prized during a period in which most dogs and people alike endured great hardships.[25] In England the rewards for this uniquely privileged status materialized early, and continued through the Renaissance, for the Forest Laws of 1016 that exempted them from ownership by poor people lasted largely unchanged for 600 years,[26] consequently bringing significant material advantages to dogs of this type. One purpose of these codes was to regulate the conditions of dog ownership, especially to address the problem of commoners keeping dogs near the royal forests, where hunting was restricted. While the Laws acknowledged the widespread utility of dogs, as well as the custom of keeping them as both pets and working dogs, they also employed the most brutal restrictions to deter poaching, including dog torture. But greyhounds apparently escaped this form of punishment.

According to these Laws, farmers and freeholders could keep large dogs, provided that they were rendered unable to run by one of several, sometimes fatal methods: hamling, hambling or hoxing (all terms for hamstringing); expediating, or using chisels and mallets to gouge out the pads from the dogs' feet; and lawing, also called clawing, which involved using chisels and mallets to strike three claws from dogs' forefeet.[27] The initial Forest Laws exempted no dogs by breed from these crippling practices, but greyhounds were spared because they, otherwise ideally suited for poaching, remained forbidden property for commoners.[28] Eventually this legal mutilation was abandoned in the face of ongoing poaching and general disgust at the enforcement of lawing. Like dog collars, which were initially developed to check dogs' freedom and later became an armour to protect them, especially from wolves,[29] these regulated forms of torture began as a bad idea for asserting control and mutated to suit the interests of dogs and humans alike. As part of this process, the growing acceptance of a concept of breed, initially an offshoot of social differentiations among humans, became also an early indicator of the problems that arose from totally identifying elite humans with breed dogs.

The sporting history of dogs in the 'greyhound family' exemplifies how these associations change over time. Along with horses and hawks, the *saluki* (again, not the members of the modern breed but the hounds of this type designated by this more generic Arabic term) became the centre of the ancient sport of coursing, variations of which in recent centuries have gained popularity in Europe and America.[30] While North African and Middle Eastern traditions did not restrict hunting with this type of dog to any type of person, medieval European hunting treatises followed the Forest Laws in expressing anxiety about the fate of these 'great hounds' in the hands of commoners. These manuals often encouraged equanimity between aristocrats and their hounds or hired huntsmen and dogs (interestingly, never among all three groups), admonishing noblemen to learn the names, voices and characters of individual dogs instead of relying on their servants to do so.[31] With the transition of hunting with dogs from economic necessity to leisure activity, this emphasis on cultivating the exceptional dog's identity and pedigree thus became more entrenched as part of the regulation of human relationships. Along with greyhounds, dogs associated with hunting carry these older associations from working to recreational contexts, so, for instance, breeds with long sporting histories such as cocker spaniels, Labrador retrievers and beagles have become popular pets.

As dog sports became more formalized during the eighteenth and nineteenth centuries, interest in hunting and racing dominated dog literature, and the noble social status and physical versatility of greyhounds ensured that they continued to be represented exceptionally well. But sporting, unlike showing, is both more and less exacting in its standards of inclusion: sporting enthusiasts more precisely exclude dogs who fail the test of performance and are less influenced by pedigrees in their breeding practices. Indeed, a common theme of sporting dog stories concerns how pedigree dogs fail where mutts succeed

Former miner John D. Eddy of Cornwall, with dogs he trained for the Butte, Montana, greyhound racing track, 1942.

(such as Sarah Orne Jewett's short story of 1899, 'The Coon Dog'),[32] often set up by the unskilled huntsman's preference for the pedigree dog (as depicted in Farley Mowatt's memoir of 1957, *The Dog Who Wouldn't Be*). The subsequent measured popularity of greyhounds as pets and contenders in the coursing, showing and racing industries derives from a combination of their history of elite association and their adaptability to such diverse roles as family pet and famous champion.

Royal ties persisted throughout the nineteenth century, prominently in the image of Queen Victoria's greyhound Hector ranged alongside other breed dogs and exotic animals in Edwin Landseer's painting of 1837–8, *Her Majesty's Favourite Pets* (private collection). The pet status here indicates

Guinefort's legacy, since the greyhound becomes a model breed dog, a favoured, loyal and even charismatic individual. But it also shows a profound social shift from working to companion status. As scent hound varieties came to eclipse greyhounds in hunting over the course of the eighteenth century, greyhounds found a new niche as heroes of racing sports, particularly coursing. Introduced into England in 1576, the European version of coursing first involved hounds chasing an actual hare across open countryside. In the twentieth century, with the adoption of an artificial hare (or 'lure') on an automated wire on a fixed, circular track, 'lure coursing' spawned a lucrative greyhound racing industry across the world. With this transition, the singular history of the greyhound became an important tool to the promoters of the industry, who stressed the breed's royal roots and companionable nature (more recently introducing on-track adoption centres), in order to gloss over the sport's current stereotypes of compulsive gamblers and exploited dogs.

Breed associations, especially with masculinity and loyalty, more clearly persist in popular representations of individual greyhounds, historic winners and fictional losers alike. Two in particular illustrate the rapid changes that the industry has wrought in the greyhound's associations from European elite sport to American seedy addiction. In the late nineteenth century, Master McGrath, the first to win the Waterloo Cup (the sport's most famous race) on three occasions, gained notoriety for appearing to demonstrate loyalty to his native Éire by repeatedly beating English contenders on their home ground, a victory commemorated by a public monument, popular song and portraits of the famous greyhound 'still proudly displayed in half the pubs and barbershops of Ireland'.[33] The most popular greyhound a hundred years later is also a male representative of his people, but more typical of dogs in the American

Monument to
Master McGrath
(died 1871),
Dungarvan, Co.
Waterford, Éire.

industry today. Abandoned at the track for losing races in the
first episode, ever since Santa's Little Helper has been the
family dog on the longest-running animated television sitcom,
The Simpsons. Remaining loyal to his unlikely saviours, the
boy Bart and his father Homer, this greyhound has prompted
satires of contemporary dog culture, from Barbara Woodhouse's
authoritarian training methods to Lassie's flawless service to
the status quo. In one episode, Santa's Little Helper even
becomes a father himself while remaining loyal to his breed,
mating with another greyhound who subsequently gives birth
to 25 champions (with cracks at Disney's animated dog films
along the way). Startling in its rarity, this image of greyhounds
having sex also shows how breed has become a way of representing the dog neither as a faithful companion nor a lewd
beast but both at once.

The integration of these meanings in the breed dog's body was familiar in Europe as far back as the eighteenth century, when it most clearly corresponded to fashionable notions of the ideal lover,[34] a concept that was influential in the development of dog fancy as a popular pastime in the nineteenth century.[35] Before this complex fusion of traditions provided the basis for the modern concept of breed, however, they were less directly linked: if the lord's faithful 'great' hound typified the faithful companion, then the lady's lascivious little dog served as his alter ego, the lewd beast. The modern concept of breed dogs as silent servants to the human structuring of their sex lives thus draws both from the ideal typified by the loyal 'great hound' and from another canine bearer of human fantasies.

As Hywel Dda's description of the 'colwyn' suggests, small dogs in feudal cultures were likewise customarily companions of the nobility. In China, the peculiar history of the Fu or Fo dog ensured that a particular kind of small dog was so identified with both courtly life and Buddhist religion that, more recently, as part of the sweeping changes of the Cultural Revolution, all small pet dogs were destroyed as symbols of decadence and corruption. But even in Western cultures, the ongoing associ-ation of many breeds in this dog type primarily with leisured women – for instance, the chihuahua Bruiser, who returns in

Maura McHugh, *The Chasing Game*, 2000, monoprint.

79

silly outfits to match his pampered mistress in the *Legally Blonde* films – points to a trend towards disparaging both that has proliferated across cultures from the early modern period.

Such associations are very old but not so consistently negative or farcical. Ceramic artefacts from ancient cultures across the Americas represent small dogs being held by women. Dating from as far back as 1500 BC, little is known about the original purpose or meaning of these images. They may indicate daily interactions or healing rituals, but all unequivocally figure 'an affectionate relationship' shared by women and small dogs.[36] The European conquest in the fifteenth and sixteenth centuries brought very different ideas about such relationships to the Americas. The clash of these traditions is emphasized in Frida Kahlo's *Itzcuintli Perro con Migro* (Itzcuintli Dog with Me, 1938, private collection), a self-portrait that depicts the artist with a little dog – named by the Aztec word meaning 'dog', which is also an ancient calendar sign associated with good luck and bliss[37] – staring back at viewers. Her clothing and positioning with the little dog here are stereotypically European, but they also conflict with the figures' indigenous American features, suggesting a native history overwritten by colonial expectations of their relationship. Neither demure nor strictly decorative, the woman and little dog here confront even as they invoke European traditions of white bourgeois feminine beauty and canine breed alike. But reading this little dog as *itzcuintli* is crucial to understanding how and why dogs gain distinct breed meanings through the interfaces of cultural histories.

The ancient sources of the European meanings in this painting stem from the Far East, where little dogs have long been associated with the movement of religion across cultures. Certain breeds legendarily were developed to embody the hybrid lion-dog, which represents the introduction of Buddhism

Frida Kahlo, *Itzcuintli Dog with Me*, 1938, oil on canvas.

within various Asian cultures: *shi zi* (in Chinese), *shishi* or *kara shishi* (Japanese), *kang seng* (Tibetan), *su tu* (Vietnamese) and *sing tow* (Thai) all refer to the fantastic animal that was converted to Buddha's *dharma* or doctrine of peace,[38] and which people tried to replicate through breeding actual dogs to look small, hairy and flat-faced. Once revered as symbols of the lion-dog, in China these Fu or Fo dogs became the provenance of emperors. Today they are most commonly claimed to be the ancestors of modern breeds said to originate as 'under-the-table-dogs' in China, such as the Pekinese, shih tzu and pug, as well as the Tibetan lhasa apso, the Japanese chin and the Maltese. This last breed, of Mediterranean origin, was traded for silk in China as early as 100 BC via Rome and (in the centuries that followed) Constantinople. But in these early European cultures, this type of dog also had special cultural meanings. An ancient Sicilian story of a lapdog, whose barking alerted a cuckolded citizen to his wife's rendezvous with her lover,[39] indicates that little dogs' affiliations with privileged women have a long and perhaps purposeful European history in the regulation of domestic affairs.

The purpose became unequivocal by the Middle Ages in handbooks for women such as the fourteenth-century *Le Ménagier de Paris* (Parisian household management), a book that exhorts its intended female audience not only to behave like a model dog – specifically, a 'greyhound, a mastiff or a small dog' – by following her husband / master and taking beatings from him gladly,[40] but also offers advice for rehabilitating a marriage after either partner's adultery. More specific connections between little dogs and affluent home economics appear in Jan van Eyck's *Arnolfini Portrait* (overleaf), where the little dog standing between young bride and wealthy merchant husband suggests how good breeding, a cultural and biological imperative, anchors the bourgeois home.[41] Interestingly, while viewers today usually read the woman in this image as pregnant, contemporary viewers would have recognized instead that she was simply holding up her dress in a fashionable style. It is possible, then, that this image connected lady and lapdog even more directly to each other, both through service to their shared master and through the associations of this kind of woman–dog relationship with childlessness that from this period on would become increasingly prevalent and controversial.

Frans Pourbus
the Younger
(1569–1622),
*Young Girl with
Dog*, oil on canvas

By the fifteenth and sixteenth centuries, writers were attributing some utilitarian qualities to lap dogs, usually concerning health, yet increasingly in the context of ladies' luxury. Notable examples include Juliana Barner's chapter on hunting in the *Boke of St Albans* of 1486, which mentions 'smale ladies popis that beere a Way the flees'.[42] More explicitly, the treatise of 1570, *De canibus Britannicus* (On British dogs), by the English royal physician Johannes Caius describes how a 'tiny breed of dog' is useful as a warm compress for relieving indigestion, affirming a long-standing folk tradition that dogs will absorb sickness and evil from the afflicted – incidentally one of the reasons why dogs were tortured and killed as the 'familiars' to their human 'witches' in the century that followed.[43] But, Caius clarifies, such a dog is primarily 'a luxurious plaything for women'[44] and (recalling the Sicilian story) otherwise useful only 'to shew

Jan van Eyck,
*Giovanni Arnolfini
and his Wife
Giovanna Cenami
('The Arnolfini
Portrait')*, 1434,
oil on wood.

up an adultery'.[45] Showing how common these associations had become by the seventeenth century, the Spanish author Cervantes conflates them in a joke as he makes the interlocutors of 'The Dog's Colloquy' unable to determine finally whether their mothers were human witches or canine bitches.[46] Through these

Today, women with small dogs signal leisure, even elegance, but they are trivialized as well as part of a longer history in which, for instance, 'pug' first meant 'courtesan' in English. A postcard for the Franco-British Exhibition, London, in 1908: *The Entente Cordiale: Marianne and the Bulldog.*

associations, the small dog especially became in popular parlance a 'comforter' or 'toy', one that is now a popular marketing tool associated with children but was once more clearly the hallmark of an unruly woman.[47]

The idea that little dogs both stand for and take the place of humans as objects of a wealthy woman's affection informs the most common derogatory stereotypes of small dog breeds. A contemporary of Barner, Geoffrey Chaucer clarifies this critique

as the narrator of his *Canterbury Tales* chides the Prioress for giving her 'smale houndes' the best food along with her own 'tender herte',[48] suggesting that these would better serve men. With the rapid growth of the merchant classes during the Renaissance, the relationships of leisured women with their small dogs became more common, and consequently a favourite target of misogynist abuse as well as class critique. Abraham Fleming, who in 1576 published a fast and loose translation of Caius under the title *Of English Dogges*, embellishes his source to add harsh words only for women who keep 'toye' dogs, an especially 'currish kinde'.[49] Fleming waxes ministerial, even poetic, as he condemns dogs of 'dantie dames' or 'wanton women's' toys as 'instruments of folly for them to play and dally withal, to tryfle away the treasure of time, to withdraw their mindes from more commendable exercises, and to content their corrupted concupiscences with vaine disport'.[50] The high rhetoric bringing together such disparate ideas of sex perversion, sociopathy and wastefulness in the image of the rich woman with a small dog would be laughable if the sentiment did not sound so current.

More than 400 years later, prejudices against people with pet dogs remain socially acceptable. While more recently the objects of such mixed feelings of 'pity or contempt' have come to include gay people as well,[51] the primary targets of this sort of abuse remain the childless and / or post-menopausal women singled out by Fleming. Some women do embrace the 'dog mom' stereotype as an affirmation of their full, rich lives with dogs, especially under the scrutiny of family and friends.[52] The trans-sexual economist Deirdre (formerly Donald) McCloskey wrote in *Crossing: A Memoir* (1999) about how the constant companionship of her Yorkshire terrier Janie (named after the novelist Jane Austen, also Donald's drag name) helped her through subsequent abandonment by wife, sister and adult children. In this story, Janie, who accompanies McCloskey even during lectures, becomes more than an accessory to this new woman's new life.

But the dovetailing of these attitudes with other forms of sexism means that many women resent being seen as a dog's 'mother'.[53] 'I am I because my little dog knows me' is one refrain that people identify with Gertrude Stein, a line from her poem 'Identity'[54] that she returned to in her critical work as an example of exactly how this process of identification 'destroys creation'.[55] Literary interpretations of Stein focus on the process that she uses to describe the notion of self-awareness (or self-influence) growing as it becomes projected through another, but, in this context, the lesbian poet's object choice ('my little dog') becomes all the more crucial to illustrate how this sense of self limits (instead of empowers) the artist. For women like Stein with no children, broader social stigmas thus continue to counterbalance the immediate advantages of canine companionship.

Other texts make the backlash even more explicit. Developing these associations amid the rise of breed, Emily Brontë's novel of 1847, *Wuthering Heights*, depicts a lady's springer spaniel both as a victim of class warfare and as a symbol of the rogue hero Heathcliff's fatal attraction. Even before his beloved Catherine dies and he marries her sister-in-law Isabella to exact his revenge on the gentry, Heathcliff for many readers proves a villain by hanging Isabella's little dog, symbolically visiting on the little dog the fate that this outcast wills for his lady. This kind of dog thus not only indicates problems with (and for) the wealthy woman, but also becomes identified with her, sharing the peculiar advantages and hazards of her social position.

Even the specific association of adultery and the little dogs of affluent women persists, both at the end of the nineteenth century in Anton Chekhov's story 'The Lady with a Lapdog' and at the end of the twentieth in the plot line following the 'home wrecker' Valeria and her 'lovechild' terrier Ritchie in the film of 2000, *Amores Perros* (Life's a bitch). The initial framing of these negative stereotypes through 'smale ladies popis' indicates how the emerging conceptualization of breed as an end in itself involves not simply a shift in attitudes towards dogs but more fundamentally towards regulating sexual relationships among humans, as well as dogs. And, as Kahlo's painting suggests, the cross-cultural histories of certain kinds of little dog chart how breed becomes a way of continuing the long human traditions of defining cultural differences through relationships with dogs.

Small dog breeds proliferated in Europe with the fad for all things exotic and especially miniature at Baroque courts. The Cavalier King Charles spaniel is one obvious example, but the displacement of so-called native European breeds by 'oriental' ones like the pug (then the favourite of Dutch courts) is telling. So familiar have these images and meanings become to Western minds that the figure of the little old rich lady's pampered Pekinese, her 'substitute baby',[56] now even inspires nostalgia. The novelist James Herriott appeals directly to this notion through Mrs Pumphrey and her Pekinese Tricki Wu, the chief featured characters among his veterinary patients in both the novel (1972–92) and the television series *All Creatures Great and Small* (1978–90).[57] Appealing to Chaucer's stereotype, the ailments of this Pekinese result from his lady's excessive indulgence, and, for treating him, Herriott's vets in turn are showered with rare treats. The little Chinese dog becomes a vehicle for an exchange between the work of the English country vets and the generosity of the otherwise alienated rich lady, his cycles of suffering thereby galvanizing temporary relief from class conflicts. This particular breed member's role as exemplary oriental in part derives from the special position of the Pekinese in the development of the modern notion of breed.

The material records of the Pekinese (or *Fu-Lin*) are perhaps the oldest of all breeds, stemming like the greyhound's from their associations with religion and royalty. Little dogs of this type, again the Fu or Fo dogs that were considered living forms of the 'spirit-lion' or 'lion-dog', were bred to approximate this symbol of the introduction of Buddhism to China during the eastern Han dynasty nearly 2,000 years ago.[58] As such, they became sacred animals; eventually, they were bred exclusively by the imperial palace eunuchs, who thereby stood to gain favour with the emperor. Select dogs were kept not as pets but as members of the court; they were given titles, guards and other aristocratic amenities, and stylized portraits of them were painted in the emperor's 'dog-books', which created a rudimentary record of the breed members as well as the visual standards for the breed. The earliest images are extremely stylized, and it was not until the Manchu dynasty in the eighteenth century that artists began to create and popularize realistic images of these dogs,[59] a shift that reflects their rapidly developing exchange in popular and foreign markets. Their export to Europe, first as court novelties in the sixteenth and seventeenth centuries and more broadly as luxury pets by the eighteenth, proved a crucial turn in the breed history of Pekinese dogs, since up to that point it was difficult to distinguish them from dogs of the pug and Japanese chin type. For only then did the breeding aesthetic change from the individual fancies of succeeding emperors, as recorded in paintings, to the show judge's preferences, limited by closed stud books and the measurement requirements recorded by breed clubs.

The institution of this new system can be traced to England with the Beachborough kennel records of 1795, which identified individual purchased foxhounds – 'the most carefully bred dogs at the end of the [nineteenth] century, although the most "mongrelly" at its outset'.[60] These provide the first documents of what quickly became the standard for canine pedigrees. The identification of a closed breeding pool in this instance supported an already established preference for a visible type, in turn reflecting the cultural conditions that enabled a shift in human-controlled dog breeding from a comparatively limited and idiosyncratic practice to a more public and popular one.

More clearly in the case of Eastern breeds, cross-cultural printing and transportation technologies augmented the dog's 'flexible, even metaphoric, nature'[61] as breed registries and more broadly popular pet fancies took shape.

Tellingly, the breed clubs that maintained such records were first incorporated in order to regulate dog shows, which started in Britain in the 1840s as somewhat shady leads (exhibitions) held in public houses. Within 50 years they had become enormous expositions attracting thousands of people with dogs at high-profile venues such as the Crystal Palace in London.[62] The first event advertised as a dog show was a small affair held in Newcastle upon Tyne in 1859, but the shows that soon followed became large and chaotic, inspiring the incorporation of societies and the adoption of precise codes of rules.[63] Formal pedigrees for most breeds were initiated by the largest of such groups with the publication in 1874 of the British *Kennel Club Stud Book*,[64] which from 1878 was reinforced by the *American Kennel Club Stud Book*. The purpose of these books was to offer both breeders and show judges a stable list of which dogs belonged to which breeds (preventing cross-listing across categories at dog shows), and eventually a definitive list of the male dogs who could officially sire 'breed' pups. The so-called noble and ancient bloodlines recorded by this institution of closed stud books were therefore quite recent inventions. They served to stabilize the economic and emotional investments of humans in dogs as much as the reproductive patterns of dogs themselves.

With the advent of dog fancy as a leisure activity and the consequent organization of breed clubs, audiences grew not only for these events but also for dog literature. This created a huge demand for new and original work. The first popular dog book in English since Fleming's translation of Caius, Sydenham

Jean-Baptiste Oudry, *Bitch Hound Nursing her Puppies*, 1752, oil on canvas.

Edwards's multi-volume but never completed *Cynographia Brittanica* (1800–05), indicates how this growing popular interest stemmed from increasing awareness of the various types of dogs. *Cynographia Brittanica* describes the dogs through anecdotes as well as natural history, and features realistic colour illustrations of them. It was the first of what became a prolific type of dog book. Adopting the popular pseudonyms Dinks and Stonehenge (the *nom de plume* of the early dog-show judge and field-sport writer John Henry Walsh), by the end of the nineteenth century many writers both promoted this interest in individual breed dogs – one goes so far as to claim that to 'form one perfect dog' is 'the great art in breeding'[65] – and acknowledged frankly that the breeding of prize dogs was rapidly becoming an 'industry'.[66] Through visual representations especially, the breed dog came more clearly into view as both a product of and a response to the social displacement and aesthetic fluctuations that characterized industrialism in an age of empire.

Franklin D. Roosevelt and daughter Anna with Chief of the Mohawk at the Seventh Annual Dog Show of the Washington Kennel Club, 1920.

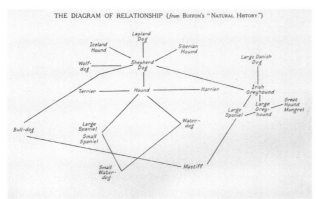

THE DIAGRAM OF RELATIONSHIP (*from* BUFFON'S "NATURAL HISTORY")

'The Diagram of Relationship' in Edward Ash's *Dogs: Their History and Development* (1927), based on one in the Comte de Buffon's *Histoire naturelle* (1755).

Jean-Baptiste Oudry's painting of 1752, *Bitch Hound Nursing her Puppies,* among the first of a popular genre, is an indication of this development. Its revolutionary content – animal mothering – is tempered by a subtle appeal to breed via uniform canine shapes and colouration. Isolated by 'dramatic luminary effects' in barn birth scenes, the clone-like puppies indicate either that their mothers are 'canine Madonnas'[67] or that their parents resemble one another closely. Either way, the painting emphasizes family in the context of breed. Significantly, the artist and his contemporary viewers were in agreement that this painting was his best work.

Ideas of the dog shifted more generally as the breed aesthetic took shape. A few years later, Georges Louis Leclerc, comte de Buffon, in his widely influential *Histoire naturelle* (1755), remarks that the dog alone, 'independent of her physical beauty, vivacity, strength and gracefulness, has all of the interior qualities that draw people to animals'.[68] As they colonized the world, Europeans found dogs living with humans everywhere. This led them to reflect, seemingly for the first time, on the significance for humans of this primary cross-species relationship. A generation later, Henry Mackenzie's novel of 1771, *The Man of Feeling*, extended the ideal canine qualities to the symbolic values of the faithful lover through the dog Trusty, who dies of sadness when his loving human family is evicted from the only home they have ever known.[69] As Oudry's painting shows, breed aesthetics subtly became part of the popular sentiments that were then changing in favour of animals in general and the dog in particular.

The dog mother and puppies were objects of sentiment, but viewed retrospectively as incipient breed members they are also an object lesson in how the breed dog contained a more volatile process of social transformation through breeding. Nobility of pedigree, constancy in form and reproductive faithfulness to one's master coalesced in an aesthetic of social reformation that seems a precise reaction to the revolutionary social turbulence among humans. But as these idealized meanings took shape, the

The 'Bichon', the 'Chien Lion' and the 'Dogue de Forte Race', from the Paris edition of Buffon's *Histoire naturelle* (1799–1805).

94

contradictions within the breed dog's body also gained greater significance. By the late nineteenth century, the keeping of a breed dog metaphorically equated the owner with the dog's supposed nobility,[70] while breeding involved a more aggressive reinvention of the social order, thus threatening the stability of such nobility.[71] Consequently, breed images of another type, the dog portrait, displaced the canine Madonna genre as the most popular way of imagining breed dogs. By the end of the nineteenth century, when photography had been increasingly perfected, this new emphasis on the individual breed dog is particularly evident in photographs of dog-show champions, who, like the human breeders sometimes included in these images, stand alone or with their adult children. Here as well, the subjects started as familiar images of loyalty and noble birth, as uniformly breed dogs who were the pets of aristocratic patrons,[72] but the focus on the individual dog characterized the growth of this genre throughout the twentieth century, becoming career highlights of artists such as the painter David Hockney and the photographer / videographer William Wegman, as well as the bread and butter of largely anonymous painters and photographers in the kitschy cottage industry of pet portraiture.

Although the images generally conceal the tension between social construction and elite identity, these problems of the canine Madonnas resurfaced notably in the 1990s, with the reinvention of the dog portrait genre by Thierry Poncelet, an artist who also works as a painting conservator. Poncelet's images are actually therianthropic palimpsests, that is, hybrid and reused nineteenth-century portraits in which breed-dog heads are painted over those of human individuals. While they lay bare the interchangeability of canine breed for human social class, these portraits of what Poncelet calls 'aristochiens' are often read as social satires,[73] even as a commentary on fascina-

Thierry Poncelet, *Woman of Qualité, Louis xv Style*, 1990s, oil on canvas.

tion with pedigrees, whether in peerage or stud books.[74] But as a social phenomenon the images have proved more complicated. Just as the show-quality dog inspires fads among pet owners and fine art, breed-dog pet portraits inspire broader trends in home decor, so Poncelet's aristochiens have inspired a subgenre of popular pet portraiture. These, like the breed dogs that

Francis Barraud,
His Master's Voice,
1898–9, oil on
canvas.

inspire them, appeal to human desires for 'historical identity or racial purity'.[75] And, just as champion show dogs rise above the average breed dog in commercial value, a Poncelet original becomes through this process a 'positional good' or a special kind of commodity whose value is determined both by its rarity and by the lack of a precise exchange equivalent.[76]

The Victoriana painting styles in this new genre also revive and reinforce the cult of the breed dog, since they recall another sub-genre within the tradition of dog portraiture, the dog mourner painting. The most famous example of this genre, and among the most reproduced paintings of all,[77] is Francis Barraud's *His Master's Voice* (1898–9), which is best known as the origin of Victor, mascot of the recording company RCA, and perhaps most visible today in the logo for the HMV Media Group. Barraud's painting of his own fox terrier Nipper, read and reproduced now as an icon of bedazzlement with new technologies, is said to represent the dog's response to hearing a recording of the artist's dead brother (interpreted as 'his master'), technologically speaking from beyond the grave. In this way it was embraced immediately in the tradition of the dog mourner, a version of the dog portrait in which an individual breed dog reclines melancholically by a coffin, corpse or even a mourning wreath, faithful to the human even beyond death.[78] As an indication of anxieties about urbanity and modernity,[79] Nipper's / Victor's pre-eminence in this genre and persistence beyond it suggest how many meanings converge in these representations of the breed dog, shaken but not stirred from this role during the digital and 'video revolution', as he now advertises CDs, DVDs and games. The genealogy of the images themselves, however, mirrors their consistently breed-dog content. One can see Barraud's image as a Realist invocation of a genre tradition that harks back to Oudry's representations of superior canine sensibilities, moving stylistically from Romanticism, as in Edwin Landseer's *The Old Shepherd's Chief Mourner* (1837, V&A Museum, London), to the Pre-Raphaelites with Briton Rivière's *Requiescat* (1888, Art Gallery of New South Wales, Australia).

An inevitable response to such heavy-handed depictions as Oudry's canine Madonna, affectionate identification with breed dogs as charismatic individuals can also be seen as central to the emerging Romanticist 'cult of the pet'.[80] Illustrative of this is the poet George Gordon Byron's epitaph for his dog Boatswain, praising 'One who possessed Beauty without Vanity/ Strength without Insolence/ Courage without Ferocity/ And all the virtues of Man without his vices.' Above all, supernatural devotion to people became the ideal canine virtue, and the breed dog, both real and imagined, became its avatar. So an actual Lake District tragedy of 1805, in which the corpse of a young man killed in a mountain-climbing accident lay undiscovered for months while being guarded all the while by his terrier bitch, became the subject of numerous popular representations in early nineteenth-century Britain, including Walter Scott's poem 'Helvellyn' and Edwin Landseer's painting of 1829, *Attachment* (private collection). Sentimental attachment even to the little dog, no longer an unclean or lewd animal but imagined here as an unquestioning and devoted companion, became justified by these more direct appeals to the cult of the breed dog. Following Oudry, Romantic artists trained their sights carefully on breed members: Boatswain, Byron insisted against the evidence, was a pure-bred Newfoundland; Landseer's canine portraits almost exclusively focus on breed dogs, including his own favourite pet, Lassie the collie; and Scott's favourite dog, Maida (also one of Landseer's subjects), was a deerhound who became 'nationally famous' through the artist's work and the tourists it attracted.[81] Reciprocally, adoring fans reinforced this identification of breed dogs with Romantic art, for instance naming a breed of terriers for Scott's fictional character Dandie Dinmont.[82] This more widespread cultural affirmation of human–canine sentimental attachments had more immediate consequences for the development of breed dogs as commodities, and bolstered the formal registration of breeds throughout the nineteenth century.

Once the breed dog took shape conceptually within the canine family tree, it also gained membership within the human family as part of the enormous social changes that characterized the rise of capital through the industrial era. In these new contexts, the paradox of breeding and breed took new form in conflicting notions of ideal canine lovers as valuable property. Such a conundrum structures Virginia Woolf's singular bestseller *Flush* (1933), her biography of Elizabeth Barrett Browning's cocker spaniel.

J.M.W. Turner, *Dawn After the Wreck*, c. 1841, oil on canvas.

The frontispiece, a photograph of Woolf's own cocker spaniel, Pinker, signals the parallel lives of these breed dogs.[83] They are not merely members of the same breed; they are also gifts to each writer from other women, symbols of friendship as well as the active companions that the women take into their married lives. Their status as highly individualized and valuable pets informs the story's central drama, where Barrett (not yet married to Browning) finally leaves her father's house to rescue Flush after he has been abducted by dog thieves.

A strangely Victorian 'tax' levied by the poor on the rich,[84] dog stealing hinged on a wealthy owner's sentimental attachment to his or her pet. But, in Woolf's reconstruction of this event, the equation of owner and pet (also by dog thief and biographer) likewise becomes inseparable from the crime. As Flush looks around him in his captivity, all the other dogs he sees are like him, 'dogs of the highest breeding',[85] suggesting that ransoming the individual is not nearly as criminal as making breed dogs targets of human class conflict in the first place. Although

Frontispiece of Virginia Woolf's *Flush: A Biography* published in New York in 1933. The 'Flush' in this photo is actually Woolf's cocker spaniel Pinker, a gift from her lover, Vita Sackville-West.

rarefied, these relationships of breed dogs, wealthy owners and poor opportunists signal the broader social contexts within which such dogs gained special significance.

For Victorians anxious about social mobility, the breed dog served as a means of securing – and as a marker of achieving – elite status in the show ring, as well as at home. More generally, national kennel clubs recorded surges in ownership of certain breeds in direct response to the circulation of popular stories and images. But, especially during the nineteenth century, the dog show set a precedent for a value system of breed that increasingly became a hallmark of bourgeois life. As a highly ritualized event meant to sanction and foster 'good breeding', the dog show seemed increasingly a strangely overt spectacle of the regulation of the bodily, especially sexual, practices that structured middle-class ideology through the period.

From Christopher Guest's 2000 film *Best in Show*.

Even in a recent film comedy like *Best in Show* (2000), which parodies some of these equivalences of political-economic and biological identity forms, the ideology of breed remains true to these objectives. The film focuses on what happens, socially and symbolically, at the highest level of dog showing, when 'best in breed' dogs go on to win the championships of their respective breed groupings and ultimately compete for 'best in show'. It argues that sentiment plays an increasing role at each level, and that free-market values are counterbalanced by a conservative family agenda. In the end, old money and new apparently fail to determine success, but a certain kind of relationship between the breed dogs and their owners does, as a borderline-indigent, straight, white, happily married and disabled man brings the family pet to victory. In his wake, single, gay and dysfunctionally married men fail alongside all the women (none of whom, interestingly, stays single) in a triumph of a working class carefully re-made in the image of bourgeois respectability. To the film's credit, the story inverts the usual Hollywood stereotype by presenting the gay and lesbian characters as neither as tragic nor as sinister as the heterosexual ones. But they all are coupled and therefore faithful to a strangely psychoanalytic 'family' form, featuring two human 'parents' with canine 'babies'.

Breeds like the poodle and komondor do not shed their entire coat annually and so are shown with their coat meticulously clipped or twisted into long 'cords', or, in this case, both.

The film clarifies how, by the end of the twentieth century, the prevalence of dog ownership and the general lack of knowledge about breed rarity meant that the show-quality dog no longer so clearly augmented the owner's sense of elite social status,[86] but nevertheless still helped to regularize identity. Predominantly seen as a household pet, the breed dog instead had come to symbolize and to contribute to the formation of the bourgeois, and, even more specifically, the nuclear family. Indicative of this development is Gordon Stables's novel of 1894, *Sable and White: The Autobiography of a Show Dog*, the first of many 'picaresque' collie stories that indicate how 'shows encourage the abuse of animals'.[87] The hero, a collie named Luath, finds happiness only in his return to his human family. This suggests how the initial popularity of breed-dog representations came to serve other causes, including the modern (and often overlapping) use of breed dogs in popular media, war and humanitarian service.

This process became even more evident in the sentimental fictions of the collie as hero or heroine of home and kennel, which was first popularized by Stables' novel, as well as by Landseer's pet collie Lassie, his constant studio companion in later years.[88] Albert Payson Terhune's 'Lad' novels embellish the traditional fiction to represent the show-champion collie as an ideal pet. But this kind of breed dog became an international icon of these qualities through Eric Knight's story of 1938, 'Lassie Come Home', the origin of what became a popular film series and even television history, for Lassie is presently the longest-running TV character. Predictably, the story that within a few years grew into the novel *Lassie Come-Home* (1940) followed a circular trajectory, which took the canine protagonist from Knight's own boyhood Yorkshire and brought her back to a happy home there.

If the author's own life of international travel and wartime service exemplifies the disruptions and self-redefinitions characteristic of modern living, then the popularity of the story he tells appeals instead to the sentiment that the breed dog now elicits, namely nostalgia for lost social orders. The same sort of

'High-class pure confectionery' from Walter Emanuel's *A Dog Day, or The Angel in the House* (New York, 1902).

longing for a time when people knew (and stayed in) their place characterizes even recent memoirs, such as Willie Morris's *My Dog Skip* (1995), where African-Americans, like the Cockneys in Knight's tale, are uneasily tolerated by the landed gentry and their respectively white / local social inferiors while the breed dog in contrast is universally welcomed. In both story and novel, Knight depicts a working-class family compelled by necessity to sell their good dog to a rich duke, but, through their combined loyalty and good works, these poor but respectable people ultimately earn their dog back, as well as the aristocrat's favour. In the novel, Lassie's movements are expanded and detailed to include encounters with a First World War veteran and the parents of a dead soldier, and this story especially heals more subtly the psychological wounds inflicted on the British people, since it serves as a catalyst that moves them from dwelling on the traumas of wartime service and post-war economic depression to create the magnanimity and prosperity of peacetime.

It is a classic dog story of love, loss and loyalty with an atypically happy ending: Lassie's place is living happily ever after with the poor family who join her in service to the nobility. More to the point, Lassie's status as a breed dog enables her to uplift while affirming the human family structure, a pattern that continues through images and stories of the breed dog championing, even protecting, the parents and children of the nuclear family that remains the only constant in the many ensuing Lassie stories. In the Lassie films and TV series that proliferated during the past century, Lassie changed her nationality from British to American and even bent her gender, since 'eight (male) collies from Pal to Howard have starred in the [conventionally] (female) role'.[89] The dog actors portraying Lassie produced still another layer of family solidarity, since their original trainer's son took over the business of producing obedient, visually consistent and likewise related collie dogs for the role. More intensely than in the dog show, the breed dog's body as film star represents while restricting breed-dog breeding, making it an all the more carefully controlled site through which increasingly middle-class, heterosexual, white and Anglo-American ideals are reproduced.

Promotional still for Daniel Petrie's 1994 film *Lassie*, showing the eighth-generation descendant of the original dog star of the 1943 film *Lassie Come Home*.

Like show dogs, dog actors became a mainstay in European and American contexts from the early nineteenth century with the convergence of public sentiment for dogs and popular interest in training them. Following a vogue for dog dramas on the stage that peaked in 1814 with *Le Chien de Montargis* (*The Dog of Montargis*), which opened in Paris and was translated and performed 1,100 times in England alone, the first live dog took the role of Dog Toby in the traditionally British Punch and Judy puppet theatre in the 1820s. Just another puppet in the previous 150 years, Toby soon 'became the most popular feature of the show' when played by an actual dog who sat on the playboard and interacted on cue with the puppets.[90] While such use of dog performers in live popular entertainment emerged from the travelling show or circus traditions recorded much earlier by Caius, the anticipation and integration of the actions of the live dog in the narrative have since become a comic mainstay of popular media.

Just as they appear widely in film and digital texts today, dogs are everywhere in early cinema, but consistently return as disruptive elements in comedy. The Edwin S. Porter film of 1905, *The Whole Dam Family and the Dam Dog*, for instance, presents a series of 'portraits' of family members standing in a picture frame, who become funny in juxtaposition with snide descriptions of them in inter-titles. Only the Dam family dog has an action role, jumping at the end through the frame and towards the camera, at once revealing and terminating the frame and camera as structuring devices. Although much more elaborately staged, a similar effect of dog action on screen assumptions can be seen in William Wegman's videos and even in his feature film of 1997, *The Hardly Boys in Hardly Gold*. Carefully dressed, the dog stars are positioned to mimic human actions up to the dramatic climax, when they drop to all fours and run, acting for the first time like dogs. As the narrator dryly observes: 'They're girls. They're dogs. They're Hardly Boys.'

But unlike the Porter dog and his own earlier canine actors, Wegman now consistently uses breed dogs, all Weimaraners. More like the Hollywood collies who have played Lassie, they are all immediate family members, pets bred by Wegman and made the focus of his art. Thus, while comic film roles for dogs can enable them to violate human expectations, and even cultivate more complex approaches to animal aesthetics (and Wegman's earlier experimental video especially illustrates this point),[91] they have come to do so within a commercial film context that increasingly privileges breed. Through this repetition, even serialization, the breed dog creates and sustains instead an exceptionally human image of 'our very own saint in the backyard',[92] repackaging the older associations with religion, nobility and nostalgia to suit new social ideals, if not realities.

Outtake still from William Wegman's 1995 film *The Hardly Boys in Hardly Gold*.

Lassie's hagiography above all relentlessly fulfils and even exceeds these 'super dog' standards. Physically strong and beautiful, emotionally available and tactful, Lassie also tutors the people she encounters; in addition to saving their lives and reconciling their differences, she teaches them especially to understand and appreciate the charms of pastoral life and noble sentiments. Moreover, a model 'friend' like the gay uncle character common to American sitcoms, Lassie has no needs – she 'never urinates or defecates', let alone comes on heat.[93] Giving everything and expecting nothing in return, Lassie has

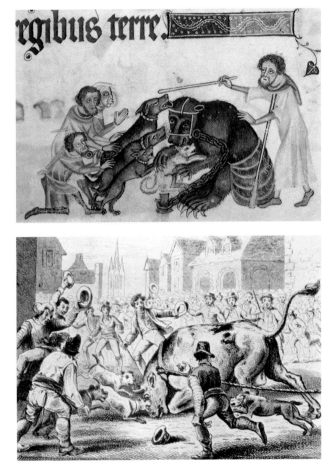

A bear-baiting scene in *The Luttrell Psalter*, an illustrated manuscript made in East Anglia, c. 1325–35.

'Bull Baiting', an etching of 1816 by Joseph Strutt.

become the 'American image of the ultimate dog', against which millions of real dogs routinely fall short and consequently end up in shelters.[94]

The idealization of the breed dog can create specific problems for popular breeds. Breed-club members lamented the demise of the Scottish collie at the end of the nineteenth century because of its popularity in Europe,[95] and similar claims were made for the German shepherd[96] in the twentieth. The mass marketing of popular media representations exacerbates this problem. Circular fads for working breeds such as Dalmatians follow the releases and re-makes of popular dog films that misrepresent them as low-maintenance family pets. Commercial successes and domestic pet tragedies alike stem from the intense marketing campaigns now centred on the release of such films, which bombard fast food restaurants, children's television programming and toy store shelves with promotional images of the celebrity breed dog.

Dogs involved in live, especially sporting entertainments, have similarly become more strictly breed-identified, but with even more profoundly ambivalent results. While the well-being of actual dogs and other animal actors involved in media production was greatly improved by industry regulation during the twentieth century, conditions for breed dogs at the centre of sports such as baiting, racing and fighting have proved more precarious. Like greyhounds in racing, animal competitors in baiting and fighting risk life and limb, while human participants largely see them as pretexts for gambling. While the most popular breeds take on special meanings over time, the histories of these leisure activities show how individual competitors sustain fatal injuries even when winning, and whole breeds bear the stigma when the sport falls out of favour.

Popular in early modern England, the sport of baiting pits dogs against other animals, typically bulls or bears with their eyes gouged out. Shakespeare historians often remind us that the Elizabethan theatre-in-the-round developed as an offshoot of these main attractions in the baiting pit. In pointed contrast to the identification of greyhounds with nobility, though, the increasing perception of mastiffs ('tie dogs' or 'band-dogs') as superior competitors in bull and bear baiting did not merit a special exemption for these breeds so much as it initiated a breakdown in the Forest Law system of mutilating them.[97] While the legal system mandated death or disability for such dogs, the sporting system only risked it, and this marginal improvement, fuelled by widespread popular support for baiting as a sport, characterized the transition of what had been a useful type of hunting and guarding dog in the centuries before reliable firearms to a popular breed of baiting dog in the early years of mass spectator sports.

Although banned along with other entertainments, initially as part of the Protestant Reformation across Europe and eventually as part of humane society and animal activist efforts around the world, organized dog fighting nonetheless continues as an underground sport. Because the sport requires less space and fewer animals than baiting, dog fighting has been much more difficult to regulate, and, even where it is illegal, 'dogmen' (the name embraced by people in this industry) find a lucrative trade in breeding and fighting their dogs. Breeds were developed specifically for this sport from the mastiffs as well as the terrier strains (many of which were created for the now defunct sport of 'ratting', in which bets were set for the number of rats that a dog could kill in a set time) that came to be known as 'bulldogs'. By 1800 Edwards's *Cynographia Britannica* could clarify how this fitful history had given rise to various national identifications, including nativist sentiments for British (as opposed to French) bulldogs.[98] Moreover, the continuing popularity of these breeds amid the rise of global poverty and urbanization led inevitably to the resurgence of dog fighting as a form of entertainment in poor urban areas.[99] As the film *Amores Perros* depicts graphically in another plot line, this sport

'How to Train a
Bull Dog' from
Sporting Magazine
(1822).

HOW TO TRAIN A BULL DOG.

typically involves two breed dogs encouraged to fight to the
death. Such entertainments are the legendary origin of 'pit
bulls' (or American Staffordshire terriers), and therefore part
of the breed history that haunts them, making them popular
urban pets and fighting dogs as well as imagined public
enemies.

In a sense, the ideology of breed turns both literally on these
dogs and less obviously on the bourgeois values of family and
sentiment, which both sides invoke defensively when the
increased visibility of certain breeds backfires spectacularly. By
the end of the twentieth century, some breeds were not only
going in and out of fashion but had also become singularly
reviled as 'avatars of the Killer Breed'.[100] Often the demoniza-
tion of a breed came as an abrupt reversal. Indeed, Stephen
King's *Cujo* (1981), a friendly St Bernard who goes 'mad' with
rabies and terrorizes a town, seems a perfect example of this
fictional phenomenon. But actual dogs were put in this position
as well. For instance, up to the Second World War the dogs now

A mid-1930s to mid-1940s promotional still for *The Little Rascals*: Pitbull Pete the Pup's head rests on Buckwheat's (William 'Billie' Thomas) shoulder.

called pit bulls were such beloved national symbols that one named Pete the Pup was the mascot of the *Our Gang* children's film series (1922–38), later broadcast from 1954 as the television show *The Little Rascals*, and syndicated and re-run for more than 20 years. As Vicki Hearne outlines in *Bandit: Dossier of a Dangerous Dog* (1991), high-profile lawsuits in the 1980s led to the pit bull's identification with urban, poor and specifically black people,[101] so that members of this breed became the object of subtle (and sometimes obvious) forms of racism. Now even suspected members of this breed are subject to controversial, breed-specific prohibitions in leases and even local ordinances that echo (and arguably become a means for reasserting) the anti-black policies common 40 years ago in the segregated US. Moreover, persecution of individual dogs as breed representatives in the name of child welfare, urban safety and even animal protection further highlights the sense in which badly behaving individual dogs do not betray the standards of a particular breed so much as they challenge the idea of 'breed' as both symbol and mechanism of social regulation. Here perception of a dog as a pit bull is what counts, not its lineage, and again for a dog relinquished by law to a shelter this breed resemblance can be tantamount to a death sentence.

The history of war dogs also clarifies how cycles of social favour affect breed dogs even as they chart national ideologies. The practice of using dogs in war has ancient roots in the empires of Assyria, Babylon and Egypt, and has been an influential focal point in military history.[102] Medieval dogs were considered so much a part of war as an institution that they were dressed in parade suits of armour.[103] But the modern historic institutionalization of dogs in war was initiated through a network of German villages that were nationally subsidized from the 1870s. Earlier, especially in Bavaria and Austria, each regiment would employ specially trained dogs to haul the big drum on wheels during parades, but this tradition was abandoned in favour of more utilitarian war dogs, who served as messengers and scouts.[104] Throughout the First World War, the breed of choice for these purposes remained open to debate, with English trainers, for instance, preferring mixed-breed dogs in war because they were felt to be less highly strung. But Germany prevailed in Europe in the number and quality of its military dog-training schools, and these inspired similar organizations in other industrialized nations.[105] And the dog breeds preferred by the German programmes remain the most popular war dogs today. However, they also gained profound associa-

'Equipt for the Trenches', a French sergeant and his dog, both wearing gas-masks, on their way to the front line in France during the Great War of 1914–18.

tions with militarism, both the laurels of heroism and the stigma of violence.

During the First and Second World Wars, the German shepherd became the war-dog breed of choice, selected for its overall performance, general climate suitability and availability.[106] A few were briefly honoured as war heroes, such as Chips, the dog awarded an American medal (later rescinded) for bravery in combat in 1943. This influence may still be seen in the prevalence of German shepherd dogs in military service. The US Department of Defense, which maintains the largest of such programmes today, advertises on its website its ongoing efforts to obtain 'quality' German shepherd (as well as closely related but more rare Dutch shepherd and Belgian Malinois) dogs to train for patrol duties. Although the US military also actively

The 'Chien Loup', as seen in the 18th century, from the Amsterdam edition of Buffon and Daubenton's *Histoire naturelle* (1766–99).

LE CHIEN LOUP.

recruits various breeds of retrievers as detector dogs, since the mid-twentieth century the German shepherd has become by far the animal most identified with militarism in the popular imagination.

For, in addition to their practical uses in war, German shepherds – known in German as *Wolfehunde* or 'wolf dog' – gained a strong symbolic association with National Socialism and the Nazi party between the wars.[107] The wolf was one of the party's popular symbols, and the codename of its leader Adolf Hitler, a notorious dog lover. This connection was reinforced through representations of the Nazi Holocaust, in which the general revulsion felt by survivors towards dogs as animals policing *shetls* (ghettoes) and concentration camps becomes embodied in the breed dogs, who in the tales invariably accompany ss officers.

A police dog attacking a man as police break up a crowd gathered outside a courthouse for the trial of sit-in demonstrators, Jackson, Mississippi, 1961.

This police dog is attacking a man during a demonstration coinciding with the arrival in Rhodesia (now Zimbabwe) of British Commonwealth Secretary Arthur Bottomley in 1965.

This specific connection and its more ambivalent ramifications for German shepherds in America are in turn exemplified in the long-running US television sitcom *Hogan's Heroes* (1965–71). Repeated episode after episode, the opening sequence of the show identifies American POWs with the Nazis' caged guard dogs, their kennels serving as part of the tunnel networks constructed by the prisoners.[108] These light-hearted, fictional images are in stark contrast to the first-hand accounts, which instead echo what have since become iconic images of historic incidents in the American Civil Rights movement and African anti-colonial movements. In image after image, uniformed white men hold German shepherd dogs who lunge, teeth bared, at unarmed black people. Taken together, however, all these images secure a historically specific meaning, the identification of this breed as a special kind of weapon that defends dominant political systems with brute force.

Such associations with (former) enemies and ousted regimes consequently led to deeply ambivalent representations of this breed of war dogs, especially in America, which, alone among industrial nations, has as yet no national commemoratives or memorials to honour the service of war dogs.[109] Contemporary with *Our Gang*'s pit bull Petey character, America's favourite German shepherd, Rin Tin Tin, was arguably a product of war, through and through. Appearing in films from 1923 to 1931 (his success was credited with saving the Warner Brothers studio from bankruptcy), the first dog actor to play 'Rinty' was French, a puppy found in a bombed German kennel by an American soldier at the end of the First World War. His descendants would repeat the role of the military dog on the American frontier in subsequent films and a television programme in the 1950s; even a magazine and a popular radio programme featured the character in the inter-war period. While these

Jannettia Brodsgaard Propps with the first son of Rin Tin Tin IV to arrive in Texas, where the Rin Tin Tin legacy and trademarks are currently maintained by her granddaughter, Daphne Hereford, who founded the ARFkids Foundation.

Front cover of *Rin Tin Tin* magazine for March–April 1957, showing Rin Tin Tin.

breed-dog actors were involved in promoting as well as conducting actual military dog training, the waning interest in Rin Tin Tin in the 1960s reflects the difficulty of reconciling the actual performance records of war dogs with more nebulous ideas about what these particular breed dogs represent in the national imagination.

By the 1970s television series used German shepherd dogs more deliberately to dramatize cultural anxieties both about the reintegration of militarily trained killers in civilian life and the reliance on 'un-American' dogs for victory. A bizarre Vietnam-era television drama *Run, Joe, Run* (1974–6) centred on a German shepherd dog, who goes AWOL and is subsequently hunted by his K-9 Corp trainer. Otherwise Lassie-like in his devotion to people, Joe is plagued by flashbacks, appearing to suffer Post-traumatic Stress Disorder. He ultimately teams up with a human drifter, but the dog proves unable to return to the military or to so-called normal life. In this way, Joe both takes the position of the disaffected veteran of an unpopular war and exemplifies the assumption behind the history of war dogs in Vietnam, who were quietly abandoned by the thousands and presumed eaten by many more starving people when the US withdrew. Perhaps the strangest aspect of the show was that it was aimed at children, with a Saturday-morning time slot and its marketing of plastic Joe dolls, complete with military accessories.

More deliberately, *The Bionic Woman* (1976–8) television series attempted to rehabilitate the breed by pairing its title character with a German shepherd dog named Max, who is similarly augmented with 'bionic' prosthetics. While the woman's bionics are rehabilitative, the dog's are more clearly experimental; by saving him from the fate of a typical laboratory experiment, she forms a rudimentary support network, a new community of technologically enhanced chimeras, initially produced secretly by the US military-industrial complex (in this case NASA) but ultimately claiming their own freedom. Even more directly than Lassie before them, these breed dogs are aimed to heal war wounds, and in the process reveal deeper questions about the conflicts of identity and culture.

Across the spectrum from military to private security, real dogs continue to be enlisted to police racial, national and class boundaries, but ideas of breed dogs perform similar tasks, even coming to represent those divisions. Italian greyhounds, Lhasa apsos and American foxhounds may have been born anywhere in the world, but their breed names announce peculiar allegiances to specific peoples or regions. And these human associations built into dog-breed names become all the more peculiar when the countries that they signify no longer exist, except in historical accounts. As is the case with Rhodesian (never Zimbabwean) ridgebacks, the recent history of a revolutionary break with a nation's colonial past seems more than a breed dog's name can bear. What such names assert instead is the historical context of the rise of breed, namely nationalism in an age of empire, but even this hardly accounts for all the incongruities of breed categories. More complexly, the name of the Chinese crested, a toy breed that gained popularity in the West even as it was categorically outlawed during the Cultural Revolution in China, asserts an idea of China that has become alien to most Chinese people, who slaughtered these dogs as representatives of 'decadence and the bad old days',[110] in which most people suffered under the rule of emperors while some dogs were treated like royalty. Breed names in these contexts not only materialize one human group's fantasies about another but also become impediments to cross-cultural understanding.

This power of breed-dog naming clarifies how the names and values of dogs like the German shepherd / Alsatian / *Wolfehunde* shift especially in the context of war. Taken together, the multiple names for the same dogs say more about people's perceptions of each other than they do about the dogs themselves. They hinge on how people read these dogs as representing certain aspects of their own relationships with other people or even historical developments across groups. Writing in the USA on the eve of the Second World War, E. B. White observed that 'in the last war if a man owned a dachshund he was suspected of being pro-German' but that in this one 'they just think [he is] eccentric'. White wryly concludes: 'The growth in popularity of the standard breeds has brought about a spirit of tolerance, almost a spirit of understanding.'[111] But the joke relies on the shared anti-German sentiment among Americans; we may learn to love ourselves through our dogs but not the people we define as enemy others. Moreover, because of their breed affiliation, in this situation such non-military, non-security dogs become categorically affected by conflicts among people.

Martial affiliations have also helped breed dogs in a more specialized way to transcend these limitations of breed. Just as Germany led the world in the modern use of war dogs, it inaugurated the now widespread training of assistance dogs for people with disabilities. After the First World War, the German government issued guide dogs to veterans blinded in service, the model for a system that has widespread social approbation in spite of its limited scale.[112] For instance, assistance dogs today are accepted in public places prohibited to all other dogs, including schools, busses and cafeterias. More immediately, breed becomes a factor in choosing to train dogs for this 'uniquely interdependent, communicative, and emotionally binding' work,[113] because, while dogs are selected above all by

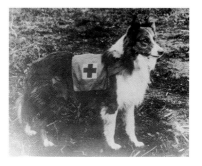

A Red Cross dog in Italy in 1909.

temperament and demeanour, to be considered candidates they have to meet standard physical size and fitness requirements; morphological breed characteristics help to narrow down the options of which puppies to target for training.

But breed dogs are also used to promote such training programmes. Reinforcing the historic breed association, Rin Tin Tin has returned in recent years to promote ARFkids ('A Rinty for Kids'), a non-profit organization dedicated to training and placing service dogs with disabled children. Only a few rare dogs and people complete such specialized training successfully to experience the benefits of such a relationship but, for those who do, the dog is, for example, 'literally experienced as an extension of the blind owner's self',[114] a complex and unique perception that also hinges on an understanding of shared human and canine identity. Informed by the history of breed, such new awareness of interdependence emerged only in the twentieth century, and the chapters that follow develop the more mixed conditions of their emergence.

Like all other significant parts of human society, human–dog relationships are thus affected by massive political and economic shifts, so breed histories, which involve long associations of canine with human types, can be read as indicators of the

Guide Dog donation receptacle, Miltown Malbay, Co. Clare, Éire, 2003.

effects of such changes within and across cultures. But, as the examples in this chapter suggest, breed both shapes and is shaped by human–dog relationships in a variety of settings, from the intimate spheres of family and home to the public arenas of sport, shows and service. The inventions of dog breeds over the past few centuries draw from and contribute to the extremes of canine physiognomy as well as the wide geographic distribution of the species. More specifically, the rising significance of dog breeds is interlinked with human societal changes, including the centralization of empire in ancient China and the commercial revolution of medieval Europe. Galvanized through the formal records of dog-breeding practices, canine breed histories intensify as well as problematize the use of dogs as powerful tools for helping people to construct and maintain social differences as part of modern industrialism.

Although of central importance to the human breeder, the documents that constitute breed – registrations, family trees, champion designations and stud books – are supplementary to the lives of dogs. As human writing for human audiences, such documents guide interpretations of the past but determine nothing of the future, not even the genetic inheritance of projected canine descendents. Dog breeds fundamentally require human involvement in a process of canine sexual selection, never predetermined but newly contested from generation to generation, a struggle that takes place within a broadly mixed social context of humans, dogs and other animals. As maps along with collective groupings are redefined in a new era of globalization, non-breed dogs – the group that has always constituted the overwhelming majority of dogs – take on a new significance in relation to the breed dog. And this potentially revolutionary force is the focus of the next chapter.

3 Mutts

Like all social elites, the breed member may be highly visible but it has always been part of a tiny minority in the overall canine population. The previous chapter began to explore this problem by showing how the rise of breed concerns human perception, never simply canine biology. But if our perceptions of breed are intricately connected with our representations of dogs – particularly idealized representations that present the breed dog as an object of affection and identification – then how do we see non-breed dogs? How does the rise of breed affect dogs who are not breed members? Detrimentally is the short answer but not a very accurate one. Zhang Chengzhi in his story 'Statue of a Dog' (2002) avoids the language of breed altogether in order to make this point: 'If global dog literature has a mainstream, it would be the boast: bragging about how one's own dog is somehow unique – smarter, fiercer and more loyal than other dogs. . . . But every dog I have ever known has been quite ordinary, common as mud.'[1] As this story goes on to show, the correspondingly low profile of the 'non-breed' dog majority, although harder to pinpoint, concerns both complex motivations and more ambivalent everyday experiences.

For Chengzhi's contrast in canine types is meant in part to illuminate contemporary problems of globalization, particularly in Asia. His narrator, a Chinese Muslim living in Tokyo, muses that the statue of the exceptionally faithful akita Hachiko at Shibuya station is a 'propaganda ploy' for non-Japanese people trying to work in Tokyo, a deceptive national breed-dog image of selflessness rewarded in a city ruled by greed. But this exemplary ruse also inspires him to recount how he witnessed a Mongolian dog so ordinary that he was called simply Jilig (dog) being saved from being beaten to death by an old woman, who threw herself over the dog to stop her neighbour from venting his prejudice against her family on the dog, temporarily frustrating the neighbour's cruel display of social power. On a day-to-day basis, dogs and people together may fail to live up to the extraordinary ideals depicted in the statue. But, in the lived experience of acting on more ordinary feeling, Jilig and the old woman indicate 'how we might create a more beautiful way of life'.[2] Indeed, the story suggests, the 'ordinary, common as mud' dog, flying under the radar of human social expectations, might be the only kind to inspire this kind of revolutionary resistance to social oppression.

However, the low profile of this kind of dog remains a problem. Even the phrase 'non-breed dog' – like all the other common terms, including 'mixed-breed', 'mongrel' and 'mutt' – for the usual products of canine self-selected breeding indicates how breed conceptually has come to colour all dogs. Within the rarefied world of the dog show, breed membership may be an individual dog's entrée to future breeding, but for the non-professional viewer it gains more widespread significance as a lens through which relationships among all sorts of dogs become visible. At one extreme, terms like mongrel and mutt make breed a kind of measuring stick, according to which most dogs fall short. Paralleling their use as ethnic and racial epithets among humans, these words imply degeneracy, degradation and ultimately social chaos, in contrast to eugenic 'hygiene', the purity or improvement promised by the controlled reproduction of breed. But even this meaning becomes unstable when applied to dogs.

These terms may be as familiar as their referent, the most ordinary kind of dog, but people using them do not necessarily believe that the non-breed dog is inferior. Instead, what these terms often indicate in casual conversation is a more complicated attempt to understand or make sense of a dog in terms of both its past and present relations with other dogs. One can interpret the non-breed / breed question as showing people distinguishing dogs from each other as well as connecting them together across breed lines, both strengthening breed as a classifying system and confronting it with the overwhelmingly non-breed dog experience. Although calculated to draw interest from consumers well versed in dog breeds, even the cutesy names of deliberate breed hybridizations – 'Labradoodles' and 'Maltepoos' – intensify the problem of fashionable breeds at the same time that they promote these mixed-breed dogs over their pedigreed relatives. Often products of increased social awareness of the health problems endemic to closed gene pools, on the one hand these new kinds of mutt indicate how sympathetic engagement has helped people to move beyond the strict confines of 'breed' to mutual canine-human benefit. On the other hand, their popularity as consumer novelties as well as their derivation from existing breed terms points to the difficulty of representing dogs apart from breed histories.

The methods involved in writing breed histories, particularly attempts to 'recover' breed origins through older representations, further distort the overwhelmingly non-breed genealogy of the dog. Unlike those of the breed dog, mongrel dog stories and images are determined not so much by physical resemblance as by negative association, increasingly with poor or homeless people and stray dogs. In European cultures, as the breed dog became an aristocrat with strong ties to family and home, his non-breed brother became an image of the early modern Everyman, associated with the more turbulent, public world of the street. Later in colonial and post-colonial contexts, such associations came to distinguish transplant from native, even white from black people.

The ancient cross-cultural histories of urban dog massacres to promote physical and spiritual health indicate how canine strays, like indigent humans, have long been identified as symptoms of social problems. While this chapter will develop why this pattern appears to have changed in recent decades, for hundreds of years mutual identification was rarely sympathetic. In sixteenth-century England, for instance, the 'dog whipper' became a regular church appointment, a post often combined with that of the beadle and, significantly, the 'bang beggar'.[3] More explicitly than altar rails, the dog whipper's job was to keep stray dogs out of church and especially away from the priests and the communion bread, both legendarily mauled by canine parishioners before such drastic measures were taken. Armed with a three-foot-long whip and dog tongs (which resemble fire tongs and were made to encircle a dog's neck for touch-free removal), the dog whipper did to dogs what the bang beggar did to humans, namely used physical force to instil ecclesiastic order. Thus connected by institutional violence, which was often administered by the same person, unruly dogs and indigent people remained the responsibility of Church authorities into the nineteenth century, when bang beggars and dog whippers were replaced by police officers and dog catchers. Thus strictly regulated by Church and later civil authorities, these canine and human groups together have long been seen as presenting ideological as well as physical threats.

This development can be traced through early modern visual art, as the ordinary dog depicted in a common place becomes a mechanism of social and cultural critique. Such a dog appears shitting in the foreground of Rembrandt van Rijn's etching of 1633, *The Good Samaritan*. Although reviled by some of his contemporaries as vulgar, this representation of a dog is more commonly appreciated as a figure of the man-in-the-street, not simply contrasting with but more importantly commenting on the more affluent title character.[4] By the eighteenth century, the role of the wandering dog in such a commentary is more often tragic, if (like images of the breed dog) inspirational to the innovation of artistic styles. In his print series, William Hogarth represents centrally in the *The First Stage of Cruelty* (1751) a gang

William Hogarth, Plate I from his engraved series *The Stages of Cruelty*, 1751.

of street boys anally assaulting a dog with an arrow, a graphic image of torture that is also striking for its early use of realism.[5] Making free-ranging dogs the object of scorn, Hogarth intimates, only institutes a cycle of violence that ultimately makes more human as well as canine victims.

These associations with abuse and public space increasingly became hallmarks of the non-breed dog in fine art, aspects that were carried over into more abstract and expressive styles of representation. For Francisco de Goya, a nondescript dog grounds a strikingly modernist and poignant painting titled simply *The Dog* (1820–23), which is frequently read as an image of Everyman in despair. The 'stray' dog's head is the only part of the animal that is visible, and its positioning at the bottom of an overwhelmingly flat, bleak canvas suggests the futility of struggle in a 'malevolent environment'.[6] Such images not only

Francisco Goya,
Perro semihundido
(The Dog),
1820–23, oil on
plaster remounted
on canvas.

contrast with the security and domesticity of contemporaneous images of the breed dog (such as Landseer's *Her Majesty's Favourite Pets*), but also more importantly represent the broad social structures of poverty and exploitation on which these rarefied social worlds of luxury and wealth depend.

If the mutt gained recognition in the shadow of the breed dog, then the institutionalization of the latter only worked to the advantage of the former, at least in popular representations. By the nineteenth century, the stray mutt had become a familiar figure of the Parisian *flâneur* (the bohemian man-about-town), significantly at a time when interest in anarchism and other extreme theories of institutional overthrow preoccupied artists and intellectuals.[7] While the poet and quintessential *flâneur* Charles Baudelaire depicted the pet dog as a figure of the foolish public – happier, for instance, with packaged shit than rare perfume in the poem 'Le Chien et le Flacon' ('The Dog and the Perfume Bottle') – he frequently wrote about his own fondness for the urban stray dog.[8] The homeless mongrel, embodying freedom of movement and especially the ability to move (and mate) among different classes, in such depictions appears not only to oppose but also actively to threaten bourgeois notions of breed.

Bringing the two kinds of dogs together further complicates the non-breed / breed representation of social stratification. In Georges Seurat's pointillist tour de force, *Sunday Afternoon on the Island of La Grande Jatte* (1884–6, Art Institute of Chicago), the black non-breed dog, eluding human lines of vision within the painting, has the sole attention of a collared and beribboned pug in the foreground.[9] On the one hand, the dogs in this painting work as a study in contrasts – bohemian / bourgeois, stray / kept, mutt / breed, dark / light – but their urban context suggests that developing this interaction can make them 'social

Georges Seurat, a conté crayon sketch for the *Grand Jatte* of c. 1884–5.

pariahs'. In one art historian's interpretation, for example, the little breed dog (ever associated with women and sex) represents 'the promiscuous, pampered prostitute, become bourgeois' and the big black mutt 'the independent, proletarian' who is also a 'possible symbol of antagonism, subversion'.[10] Leaving gender projections aside, the pug's fixation on the mutt models the broader urban preoccupation with the idea of an unstable bourgeois, even falling aristocrat, imperilled by this attraction to another who is both taboo sexual partner and social adversary. The pug's historic association with China also adds layers of ethnic and racial difference to the social dynamics in this painting. All these readings develop the mixed cultural contexts of the rise of breed, adding meaning to the wandering mongrel dog as a figure of social tension, even class critique. Although such associations may not improve the stray's condition, overall these images cast this kind of dog in a special role, signalled by the development of Realist, Impressionist and Modernist art styles, that inspires people to imagine if not 'a more beautiful way of life' then radical alternatives to the status quo.

C. G. Bush, engraved sketch of 'Arrested Rag Pickers in City Hall Park' from *Harper's Weekly* (6 July 1867).

In these images, the non-breed dog initially served as a figure of ironic contrast or chance, especially random public violence, but over time these meanings came to intersect with and illuminate other human experiences. Whether as national hero or pampered pet, the breed dog came to stand for the way that things were, but correspondingly her non-breed sister gained new meaning as well, often indicating the way things should (and shouldn't) be. Usually as an exemplary victim but sometimes the star in her own right, the mutt came to the fore in the histories and literatures of social protest, particularly in the transition from the nineteenth century to the twentieth. Sporting or show-champion breed dogs may become attractive to own because they make their owners feel richer, stronger or otherwise favourably socially entrenched in changing times, but in the process common non-breed dogs anchor critical perspectives. By the twenty-first century, the mongrel dog has become a cross-cultural trope, a more literal underdog that is especially valuable for combatting the mechanisms of social oppression. In this way, the mutt has become a powerful tool not simply for augmenting human identity but also in some instances for creating new models of the self and society.

Identification with the mutt becomes all the more interesting in light of the many barriers to this development. In the previous chapter, numerous examples underscored the ways in which identification with breed dogs can be a contradictory and disorienting process. As dogs become perceived more generally as pets, individuals who are cared for by and more broadly associated with specific people, the same process that enables owners to feel socially elevated by their breed dogs threatens to backfire on people similarly identified with non-breed dogs. A creature with little or no monetary value, who represents canine not human sexual selection and whose mixed or unrecoverable past parallels those of the so-called degenerate races of people (also identified only to be denigrated during the Ages of Reason and Sentiment), the mongrel dog symbolizes even as it stakes out the limits to this process of seeing ourselves as well as other people in dogs.

These complications come to the fore in the first novel to feature an explicitly non-breed dog as a major dramatic character, Frederick Marryat's *Snarleyyow; or, The Dog Fiend* (1836–7), a mutt who is as loved by his owner, a villainous ship's captain, as he is otherwise universally despised. As in Hogarth's image, the persecution of the mutt here is heinous: the novel graphically details for comic effect how the ship's crew members visit their own sufferings on Snarleyyow, putting out his eye, chopping off his tail, attempting to drown him and bury him alive, and in the end hanging him while pirates hang their captain. Identification of the mongrel dog with his treacherous master is unequivocal – 'They were damnable in their lives and in their deaths they were not divided' – and initiated by the captain himself, who in a surprise twist thereby becomes more sympathetic. Passion for this disfigured, mean and disease-ridden cur creates depth in an otherwise shallow villain, 'a gleam of sunshine' that is 'almost ridiculous' in his otherwise unredeemable life.[11] From one perspective, this mutt symbolizes the worthless man but, viewed another way, the dog proves the catalyst for developing something worthwhile in his owner. This profound mixture of associations, akin to the tension of breed and breeding, offers insight into the profound popular feelings that such unprepossessing dogs have come to inspire.

Sentimental visions of dogs may typically fuse loyalty, lust and higher social status in the breed dog, but these developments also have repercussions on the more ordinary ways in which people come to see themselves with dogs. In this light, the increasing revulsion for the English early modern custom of expediating ('lawing' dogs) indicates how people not only started to accept the idea that they owned dogs as property but, more importantly, envisioned even dogs in the street as representatives or extensions of themselves, if not beings entitled to protection from state torture. As these ideas took root, people became more forcefully resistant to such brutal treatment of dogs as a public nuisance. For instance, whereas organized slaughters of urban dogs were common (especially during rabies outbreaks) throughout the eighteenth century, an abrupt shift is visible in early nineteenth-century New York, where a similar action to enforce a law banning unleashed dogs (and un-penned hogs) caused a riot.[12] This identification becomes more complicated, even enabling unprecedented alliances across groups of people, when it popularly focuses on a singular mutt.

In the history of the anti-cruelty movement, a particular incident involved identification with a particular dog in ways that led socialists and suffragettes to unite briefly in London's Battersea district (the location of a large-scale and popularly supported dog shelter) in 1906 amid demonstrations collectively termed the Brown Dog Riots. In this instance, the customary class opposition of bourgeois-identified feminists and organized male workers was overcome by their shared interest in a monument to a particular victim of vivisection, inscribed to the 'Brown Terrier Dog Done to Death in the Laboratories of University College'.[13] The monument itself, like the statue of Greyfriars Bobby, included drinking fountains for humans and animals, an aspect that could have sparked a battle between its wealthy sponsors and poor residents of the neighbourhood, who had pulled down a similar one because they thought it promoted the (to them) effete affectation of temperance at the risk of the working man's right to drink alcohol. Instead a third group, the medical doctors and students who killed and reputedly tortured the dog, inspired solidarity among the memorial's sponsors and recipients. After violent clashes over the course of

A procession in London, c. 1910, to oppose vivisection. The 'Brown Dog' was one specific animal chosen to symbolize many others; a statue to it was put up in south London.

a year led the city officials to order the removal of the monument, the tenuous coalition fell apart. But the way that the dog was ultimately remembered proved significant. Although the monument described him in generic breed terms as a 'Terrier', the popular name for the incidents designated the animal only by his colour – as the 'Brown Dog' – suggesting instead a non-breed status that in part mirrors this unique, even mongrelly political alliance among human groups. In other words, this dog's posthumous associations with public space, violence, homelessness (or strays) and class difference over-determine his breed status, practically necessitating his popular reinvention as a mutt.

By the end of the nineteenth century, this imagined linkage of non-breed dogs with strays had affected the condition of pet mutts, perhaps all the more readily because ideas about 'worthless' people coloured these relationships. Anti-cruelty literature of this period reinforces the idea that the non-breed canine is both an animal victim and a figure of more broad social oppression. The first Canadian bestseller, Marshall Saunders's novel *Beautiful Joe* (1893), demonstrates how non-breed dogs serve both the anti-cruelty cause as well as the growth of women's political awareness at the turn of the century. While some writers at the time provided powerful critiques of these conditions by likening the roles of women to those of pets (especially caged birds), Saunders's novel develops how the identification with mongrel dogs serves also as a catalyst for women's work as social activists. While this more overtly sympathetic appeal gains in terms of solidarity among animal welfare and women's rights workers, the novel's strictly bourgeois context points to further problems with stabilizing this connection.

'Beautiful Joe was a real dog and "Beautiful Joe" was his real name', wrote Saunders in the preface to her historical fiction

139

P. D. Johnson,
Votes for Women,
1913, drawing.

about a mutilated mutt who finds salvation in a middle-class minister's family. Starved and beaten through his early life, Joe was rescued when his original owner, a poor and shiftless milk-man, was caught 'punishing' the dog by chopping off his ears and tail with an axe. Told from the dog's perspective, Saunders's version of Joe's story celebrates his faithful service to his new family not in spite of his having been tortured but, surprisingly, because of his non-breed status. Although his new 'mistress' Laura defensively claims that mongrels 'have more character than well-bred dogs', Joe echoes popular opinion as he dismisses himself: 'I am only a cur.'[14] The title of this chapter, 'Only a Cur' – also the title of a song popular among the children's auxiliary of the Society for the Prevention of Cruelty to Animals[15] – both names the book's primary audience and the central prejudice it aims to dispel.

Two Children Fighting over a Dog, from an undated book of *Bilder Aus Der Jugendwelt.*

The bulk of the novel develops this point: the world that Joe inhabits is generally cruel but especially so to non-breed dogs. And it frames animal abuse as a problem not simply of individual ignorance or neglect but of greed, envisioned here as a more widespread social plague visited on so-called worthless mutts like Joe. Laura learns, particularly through train travels with Joe, that the cruelty he endured and she abhors is widespread, compounded by capitalism, and best confronted through public activism. In thus leading the young woman to a vow of public service, the dog clearly bridges a generation gap, characterized by her mother's Victorian bourgeois ideals of the home as the feminized moral centre of the masculine capitalist universe and

A still from James Clark's 1959 film *A Dog of Flanders.* Note the same dog actor featured in the next image (p. 144).

the daughter's emerging world of women's suffrage, organized labour and the social regulation of industry. Unlike *Dog of Flanders* (1872), which a generation earlier had despaired of the ordinary draft dog Patrasche and his buddy, the exploited child labourer Nello, finding justice in this world, *Beautiful Joe* in this way offers a hopeful image of the non-breed dog as a source of inspiration for social progress, flagging a new potential for the mutt. Still Saunders's own fictions – she dropped her given name Margaret and pretended to be American when first submitting this book, both to gain wider readership – are telling.

Part of the mutt's value in early twentieth-century social activism derived from his utility in rooting hybrid identities, notably Anglo-American masculinity during the closing of the western frontier. The stigma of worthlessness, ugliness and randomness haunts the non-breed dog, tempering this potential for change and more directly preventing him from reaping its benefits. However, these qualities also make the male mutt the perfect foil with which the human ethnic 'mongrel' man redefines himself as an Anglo-American. So, for instance, the environmentalist pioneer John Muir wrote in *Stickeen* (1909) of initially shunning the mutt, 'so small and worthless',[16] who later shares a near-death experience on a glacier and subsequently becomes for Muir's narrator a paragon of sympathy, opening 'a window' into the feelings of 'all my fellow mortals'.[17] This revelation, however profound, inspires no loyalty from the narrator, whose departure from Stickeen and the dog's subsequent disappearance at the end of the story are as random as their meeting. In this story the mutt has no inherent value but, at a time when ethnic 'others' are less available and amenable to such appropriation, proves a useful tool in representing this new-found appreciation for the redemptive qualities of the American landscape, then newly ethnically cleansed.

Within the story Stickeen is named for the Native American tribe who first recognize how special this little dog is, an association that reinforces how the mutt takes the place of the Indian popularized in the early nineteenth-century 'Leatherstocking' tales of James Fenimore Cooper, similarly helping the white man to find himself in the rugged American landscape yet quickly dispatched when he gets too close. After 50 bloody years of genocide (loosely termed the Indian Wars), the position of Native peoples in relation to whites seems more ambivalent than this diminutive mongrel's at the time that Muir was writing. Even so, the actual dog's active role in shaping this experience, like that of the Stickeen tribespeople before him, becomes reduced to a prompt for the white man's reflections on finding himself in the wilderness.

This pattern of selective appropriation becomes all the more apparent when the mutt dog alone represents the man. Also written in America at the turn of the century, *Call of the Wild* (1903), Jack London's story of the mongrel hero Buck, parallels Muir's as a typically Victorian fantasy of men's moral improvement through contact with the wilderness – 'regeneration through regression', in popular parlance – until the end, when Buck turns away from human civilization to live with the wolves.[18] Like the fantasies of dogs as tamed wolves, London's novel hinges on the belief that the dog is primarily a puppet of man; Buck has the choice of heeding the 'call' of the wolves only when his human companion dies, an act in which the very 'last tie was broken' and, more explicitly, 'the claims of man no longer bound him'.[19] Following the conventional reading of the story as autobiographical, Buck's departure into the wilderness only reinforces Muir's point, namely that the mutt's value lies only in representing the singular experiences of the white man on the American frontier. Again like Native peoples, he is

A still from Robert Stevenson's 1957 film *Old Yeller* (1957).

imagined not as murdered, betrayed or justifiably vengeful but more conveniently as fading into the background and, in spite of his urban origins, 'returned' to nature.

This image of the mongrel as a creature of American nature makes such a dog appear even more expendable by the mid-twentieth century. For instance, the title character of *Old Yeller*, both Fred Gipson's novel (1956) and Disney's film version (1957), arrives on the farm out of nowhere, causes trouble and, although he begins to redeem himself, his triumphant proof of his worth also brings him back into lethal contact with the wilderness. The mutt saves the family from a rabid wolf only to be killed by them for having become infected with the disease. Yeller thus takes on the traditional role of the stray mutt, tolerated while useful but executed when he becomes an abhorrent disease carrier. The Disney film offers the hope that the trust and approbation he has earned will be passed on to his son, Young Yeller. But the novel offers no such reassurance and consequently novels like *Old Yeller*, particularly because they target children, are more conventionally read as positioning man's best friend as a transitional marker between nature and culture or boyhood and adult life. So expendable are dogs more generally in this *Bildungsroman* vein that the smug pubescent protagonist of a recent novel quips: 'Go to the library and pick out a book with an award sticker and a dog on the cover. Trust me, that dog is going down'.[20] But reading books like *Old Yeller* in the tradition of mongrel representations suggests a more compelling reason why in the end these dogs rarely make it out alive.

Well into the twentieth century, these associations position the mutt not only as an unlikely hero but also almost exclusively a male dog. In part, the mutt's physical ugliness serves as a ruse for the beauty of his character. The non-breed dog's usefulness comes as a surprise, a revelation of 'true' character that not only contrasts with the breed bitch's – which is expected, seemingly a mechanical function of her breeding – but also qualifies him to become the bitch's lover, the Underdog to her Polly Purebred (the canine Superman and Lois Lane characters of the animated television series *Underdog* of 1964–73). Also clarifying the increasing preponderance of females in the breed stories and images – or 'why Lassie is a bitch'[21] – these associations correspond directly with racist fantasies of miscegenation, particularly the fear of white women's seduction by black men. While the Civil Rights Movement was making literal human images of these notions politically inexpedient in the US, stories coupling breed bitches with mutt dogs became a way of keeping them in the public eye. Bringing together older associations of little breed dogs with especially sexually deviant bourgeois women and male street mongrels with proletarian or anarchist men, the Disney animated film of 1955, *Lady and the Tramp*, also subtly reflects the assumptions of segregation, since it makes the mongrel male Tramp the active seducer and the breed bitch Lady his follower or pawn.

Towards the end of the twentieth century, the mutt dog's story, as exemplified by the film of 1974, *Benji*, no longer stands in the shadow of breed dogs. But the consistently male gender of this canine character fits the centuries-old patterns of representing strays and mutts. In the *Benji* films, female canine actors play this male non-breed stray, who like many recent film animals follows the breed dog's lead in bringing together a fractured human family against the odds. Again and again Benji demonstrates that he is a desirable family pet, ensuring the character's overall pro-dog and especially pro-mutt message. Most recently through the search for the new Benji (who was rescued from a shelter in Gulfport, MS), the character's creator, Joe Camp, continues to champion the desperate cause of abandoned dogs, numbering in the millions every year in America alone. With the focus on families in the films, this affirmation of non-breed dogs becomes more squarely set within a context of social reform.

But the lived contradictions of the actors playing this character indicate their broader potential threat to the status quo. The inverse of Lassie, Benji continues to be a male character

Hoosier.

A still from Joe Camp's 1974 film *Benji.*

played by female dogs, a circumstance that caused the former First Lady, Barbara Bush, to write in *Millie's Book* about her bitch's (and her own) disappointment upon meeting the canine mutt star.[22] Prejudice seems predictable in *Millie's Book*, which explicitly contrasts family 'bluebloods' with the random 'mutts'.[23] But Bush's assumption that a mutt is socially accept-able only when both famous and male offers a rare glimpse of the human / canine intersections of gender and 'breeding', more broadly construed. For Bush, the *flâneur* lives in Benji's character, but the bitches playing him in principle prove far less charming.

Through the late twentieth century, however, the non-breed dog-in-the-street representations multiplied, enhancing tradi-tional associations with social critique. So, for instance, Jacques Tati's title character in *Mon Oncle* (*My Uncle*) (1958) is shadowed throughout the film by the family dog, likewise moving back and forth between the sterile, affluent modern home and the more traditionally gritty city life. Whereas the human invari-ably encounters problems, risking alienation with every social interaction, the dog is generally welcomed by people and by the hodgepodge pack of dogs seemingly always roaming the neigh-bourhood. Here a radical democracy of the dog world seems a utopian alternative to the constant human frustrations with technology, but it is also an image of a free society similarly hemmed in by the modern industrial world. Just as Tati's char-acter finds steady employment only far away from his family, the family dog returns every night to his food at the price of isolation from other dogs.

By the early 1970s, as radical politics gained broader audi-ences, the rare female mutt provided an opportunity to develop feminist critique. Taeko Tomioka's short story 'Scenery Viewed by a Dog' (1974) subtly incorporates a dog's perspective to mutate a comedy of manners into a woman's consciousness-raising experience. The story focuses on the housewife Chizuko, whose traditional Japanese sense of politeness is manipulated by her distant cousin and would-be suitor Hisae; precisely because Hisae has no reason to visit me, she tells her husband, I cannot tell him not to visit. But the prolonging of this failed intimacy quietly turns ugly when, on one of Hisae's pointless visits, they encounter a pregnant brown dog in Chizuko's neighbourhood. Whereas she takes pity on the dog, Hisae makes a strange comparison between puppies and severed heads, intimating violence against female dog and human alike. Viewed by a dog, the scene that unfolds looks all the more scary because nothing further happens; Chizuko becomes suddenly very afraid but she remains unable to tell this creep to leave her alone. The brown dog becomes not simply a point of comparison with the woman but also a witness to her danger, provoking and contextualizing the stalker's psychological abuse. Tomioka thus suggests a new approach to mongrel dogs not only as reflecting but also actively shaping the worlds around them.

As several examples have so far suggested, representations of multiple dogs open up this potential. This becomes particularly clear through stories of racial segregation, where non-breed dogs become a significant part of the scenery as well as characters in their own right by developing the unspoken terms of the human relationships at the centre of the story. Through the modern war-dog training programmes, actual breed dogs become involved in policing social differences among humans and in the process come to symbolize as well as demarcate cultural boundaries. Some representations of human and canine relationships with these dogs moreover make explicit their importance to ideologies of the human.

In an extreme example, the narrator of Xaviera Hollander's *The Happy Hooker* (1972) describes her attempts to seduce a white family's German shepherd during a visit to South Africa, where her strict observation of the 'colour line' categorically excludes the only human men around her, the black household servants, from her sexual interest.[24] This passage was deleted from the revised 1987 version of the book – ironically touted as Hollander's 'finally unexpurgated account' – arguably because it represents too graphically the old fantasy of idle women's sex perversion, familiar to the 'comforter' or 'toy' breed dog histories.[25] But another reason for this significant revision may be the scene's explicit substitution of breed dog for white man, an equation cast here as an inevitable consequence of anti-miscegenation laws.

These equations become unequivocal, however, through the contrast of non-breed and breed dogs. Living manifestations of South African apartheid, in Nadine Gordimer's novel *A World of Strangers* (1958) the pet dogs in white neighbourhoods bark at black people – 'You don't have to teach them; they know'[26] – while the stray non-breed dogs in the black townships bark at the novelty of white people passing through. Paired with breed dogs, mongrels not only reflect existing social inequities but also point to other social possibilities. Often the more hopeful moments in such stories concern the ways in which divisive human ideologies fail to segregate dogs themselves. Romain Gary's novel *White Dog* (1970) makes this point through the narrator's first encounter with the title character, a specialized kind of breed dog who has been expertly trained to attack only black people on sight, by presenting the 'white dog' (again a German shepherd) as initially befriended on the street and brought home by his own family's mutt. The white dog may have been trained to serve as a tool for humans, expressing and enforcing their racial bigotry toward black people, but, when turned loose on the world, he prefers the company of a mutt.

The reasons why contrasts of non-breed and breed dogs work so well to articulate and critique racist psychology become even clearer in stories that contextualize these ideas as integral to the political economies of colonialism and imperialism. J. M. Coetzee's novel *Disgrace* (1999), in which the white South African English professor David Lurie loses his job after being accused of sexually assaulting a student, and consequently moves to his daughter's farm, uses contrasts of breed and mongrel dogs to show how this man sows and reaps the systematic brutality of institutionalized racism even in the post-apartheid period. Shortly after the move, Lurie is beaten and his daughter gang-raped by their black neighbours, but his daughter refuses to prosecute or flee. Instead, she decides to keep the foetus conceived in the rape and asks her outraged father to leave.

The violator now himself violated, Lurie clings to the only work he has found in the country, helping a vet to euthanize the local mongrels who are 'brought to the clinic because they are unwanted: *because we are too menny*'.[27] Ever the English literary scholar, Lurie here recalls Thomas Hardy's novel of 1895, *Jude the Obscure*, in which a misspelt suicide note is left by Father Time, the child who kills his siblings along with himself in order to free their indigent parents of the burden of feeding them. The historic ironies of identifying impoverished Victorian children with contemporary African stray dogs may be lost on the character Lurie but not on the novelist Coetzee, who clarifies that this extension of sympathy is both an accomplishment and the racist limit of Lurie's growth.

Throughout the novel, Lurie sees black people (to him, simply 'Africans') in terms of these stray mongrel dogs – threatening in their faceless populations, marking territories and, particularly through his daughter's experience, ganging up as males to mate with a single female – and in pointed contrast to the 'thoroughbred' breed dogs he associates with white people. While Lurie's own race hatred seems to surprise him when it surfaces, these canine associations make it more obvious to the reader, in part because these uses of non-breed and breed dogs have become a metaphor for tensions between colonizer and colonized.[28] Exemplary in this vein is Ngugi wa Thiong'o's *A Grain of Wheat* (1967), which conflates racial whiteness with European breed dogs to show how such dogs have come to serve white colonial ideology even better than they physically protect their masters: the main character Koina, turning from black houseboy to soldier, returns to his white employer to kill her bullmastiff – an act that he thinks will frighten her into finally leaving his country – but later he sees her still in Kenya accompanied by another, nearly identical bullmastiff. This image clarifies how, for Koina, political revolution has brought about little social change, and it is echoed in Coetzee's novel by the English bulldog Katy, who remains with Lurie's daughter, the only one of her kennel of white people's breed dogs to survive the attack, and serves more as a sign of persistence than a mechanism of protection.

As in Gordimer's novel, the non-breed /breed dog difference initially works as a sign of social contrasts, but here mongrel dogs more actively come to undermine this division. Coetzee's conclusion, with Lurie embracing his new life as a stray mongrel 'dog undertaker' or 'harijan'[29] (literally 'child of God' and a euphemism for 'untouchable' coined by Mohandas K. Gandhi), suggests that caring for these dogs gives him a way of beginning to take social responsibilities seriously. But the change that these mutts effect in him is extremely limited. The breakdown of associations between dog breed and human racial status comes as part of the larger dramatic progression of this white African man's social worthlessness; he is progressively presented as callow lover, abusive then jobless professor, ineffectual to the point of unprotecting father, and ultimately racist white man in a predominantly black country. While Lurie's growing sympathy for the unwanted mongrel dogs seems, like that of Snarleyyow's master, a gleam of sunshine in his otherwise worthless life, his actual role – holding them while they are killed and then burning their bodies – bodes ill for his social rehabilitation and more broadly that of post-colonial cultures.

These mixed human and canine histories become a way of representing ideological conflicts and thus of rewriting histories of colonization not simply to account for multiple perspectives but more importantly to critique and ultimately change the status quo. The identification of Aboriginal peoples with dingoes, who are overwhelmingly hybrids of wild native and feral European breed dogs now on the Australian continent, pinpoints these more suggestive breed / race associations. One anthropologist notes how, when the Yarralin people of north-central Australia say that whites have 'treated them like a dog', they are both critiquing white people's relationships with dogs in contrast to their own and asserting how their own traditions are more equitable: chaining, shooting, poisoning and euthanizing are all things that only whites historically have done to dogs and to Aborigines.[30] At the crossroads of human traditions, the survival of cultural memory is inextricable from the struggle to maintain different relationships of people and dogs.

Representing the interconnectedness of these histories, B. Wongar's *Babaru* (1982) links stories of an Aboriginal man's relationship with Warand (his dingo) and of the dingo's subsequent shift from vermin to endangered species in the eyes of whites. In the first story, '*Warand*, the Dingo', the dingo caught in a leg-hold trap reminds the narrator of her *duwei* (her late husband), who was chained to a rock and left to die; both are tortured by whites, who thereby aim to exterminate them and their kind. But the story instead asserts their persistence: the *duwei* dies but returns accompanied by the ancestors in his wife's dreams and *Warand* chews his leg off to return to the bush. Rather than seeing them as exterminated, the woman sees dog and man as having escaped.

'Five Dog Night', told from the dingo's perspective, likewise recalls the suffering of his chained master in retrospect, after the dingo has been trapped and tossed into a kennel full of breed dogs where he sees another dingo eaten alive. Ostensibly spared the same fate by the white warden's new-found ecological sensibility, the dingo confronts this revised vision of himself as a symbol of the vanishing wilderness with the traditional notion of dingoes and Aboriginal people as eternal family members. Only prolonging the inevitable, however, ecology fails from this perspective because it fundamentally separates dog and human. In the end, instead of seeing himself as trapped like his people in a hostile situation dominated by Europeans, he elects to join them, starving himself to death in order to vanish beyond white control into the spirit world. The embrace of irreducibly human and canine histories – not creating new readings of present situations – delivers the dingo from this literally dog-eat-dog world. When differences among dogs are seen not simply as paralleling those among humans but as more complexly involved in shaping shared cultures, this can mean the life or death of ancient traditions.

Representations of mixed non-breed / breed, stray / mutt sexual relationships likewise radically disrupt conventional ideas about dogs as separate from (and dominated by) humans,

An early representation of a dingo, from Wilhelm Haacke and Wilhelm Kuhnert's *Thierleben der Erde* (Berlin, 1901).

even fostering new models of sex and identity. If breed dogs have come to figure modern human social hierarchies, the mongrel in turn holds out the possibility of their dismantling, in part because such a dog embodies canine self-selected breeding (as opposed to human-directed breed-dog breeding). But it is rare for a dog story to addresses this process directly. The animated film *All Dogs Go to Heaven* (1989) typically casts the mutt puppies as evidence that their German shepherd father is at best a rogue hero; by mating with and abandoning their collie mother, the roving breed dog becomes an all-too-human object lesson in bad parenting skills. Even when the Tramp is a breed dog, he is no match for a Lady, let alone a canine Madonna, so long as the dogs are imagined as reflections of humans.

More rare still are stories that explore what happens to humans who take an active role in breed- and mutt-dog breeding. Such a one is J. R. Ackerley's *My Dog Tulip* (1956), a very funny and challenging narrative of the gay male narrator's attempts to 'marry' his German shepherd bitch to another breed dog, a process that leads him ultimately to question his own assumptions about sex and identity. Queer ideas of free love and public sex hover at the edges of the text and for a few fleeting minutes are realized by Tulip and the free-ranging mongrel she chooses as her mate. But, as Ackerley describes how the mongrel pups produced through the blissful union of this Lady and Tramp lead horrible, short lives in contrast to their breed mother, his own initial prejudice turns on him with a vengeance. In short, this text shows someone who had once prided himself in being open-minded about all kinds of relationships telling an honest, if at times harrowing, tale of how he finds himself led by repressive ideologies of breed to the point at which he and others are coercing and even brutally forcing breed dogs to couple. The puppies that he so desperately wanted to enrich his breed bitch's life fare the worst of all and, through this story, these mutts become not so much a metaphor for human relations as a mechanism of the ongoing struggle to affirm social difference.

If sex with the mutt proves problematic for Tulip and deadly to her pups, then loving the mutt can lead only to disaster. Such anyhow is the premise of Anita Desai's story 'Diamond Dust' (2000), which develops the doomed passion of Mr Das, an elderly Indian man, for the mongrel dog he finds and ultimately loses on the streets. Drawn in many ways like Tulip, the mutt dog Diamond is styled even more unsympathetically: destructive, snappish, un-housebroken and faithless, this dog – 'a full-fledged badmash, the terror of the neighborhood'[31] – appears to have no qualities that justify his master's unwavering devotion. But the horror this love in turn inspires makes the human world of Diamond and Mr Das all the more repugnant. Mrs Das, driven to distraction by having to re-route her servants to pick up after the dog, intimates that the dog will be the end of their marriage. Mr Das's co-workers, 'reputable government servants' like him, disparage his new-found happiness and youthfulness when playing with Diamond as unbecoming, even symptomatic of madness. And his neighbours, already furious about the dog's habit of biting, shun him when their children find the dog engaged in sexual intercourse in the street with another stray.

In the end, no one offers sympathy when the dog disappears and Mr Das wanders the streets inconsolable, only to find Diamond in the dog catcher's truck. Running after the truck in traffic, Mr Das is hit by a car and dies, as the dog surely will in custody. A familiar ending to Indian stories about love across caste, the demise of this cross-species relationship between bourgeois man and mutt dog says as much about why human relationships have become unfulfilling for him as it does about how the regulation and enforcement of propriety and decorum in industrial, here post-colonial, societies extends through animal bodies as well. Mr Das is not so much tainted or deluded by the object of his desire as he comes to identify with the dog as a social pariah, if not outlaw. But the message is profoundly mixed. If he becomes profoundly empathetic to doggy people, he does so at the risk of seeming just plain pathetic to those who find nothing appealing about his unconditional and ultimately self-destructive love for his dog. In the tradition of *Snarleyyow*, the equation of mutt and man may help others to be more critical of the society that condemns them but it does not lessen their suffering.

To see dogs and people together as more than substitutes for each other requires a profound shift in sensibilities towards understanding shared human-canine histories, which grows through stories that emphasize the many similarities between the lived conditions of outcast dogs and homeless people.[32] If

Jean-Léon Gérôme, *The Dogkeeper*, 1876, oil on canvas.

images and stories of each have long have been a compelling subject for social critique, by the end of the twentieth century representations of the two together modelled alternate systems that proved not only more equitable to both groups but also demonstrated how they had become stronger together. Reflecting this development, the third plot line of *Amores Perros* focuses on El Chivo, an apparently homeless man who cares for stray dogs but his past, like that of the fighting Rottweiler he nurses back to health, returns to shatter the notion that he is helpless. Instead of just illustrating social problems, these human-canine relationships also serve as a basis for imagining other possibilities and, perhaps most importantly, the steps involved in their realization.

Mr Bones, the homeless man's mongrel at the centre of Paul Auster's novel of 1999, *Timbuktu*, shares the double economic burden of being socially valued as worthless and the immediate day-to-day problems of desperate living. Although Mr Bones always remains loyal to Willy G. Christmas, the man who raises him, he is also always aware of Willy's mental illness and their consequent dependence on other people, problems that become exacerbated for the dog when Willy dies homeless and the dog becomes a stray. His fortunes seem to change when a suburban family adopts him, but this experience instead grounds a broader social critique. At first, Mr Bones, renamed Sparky, experiences the freedom from material want and begins to suspect that his former master railed against these things because he had never experienced them like 'Sparky' as an insider. But as the tense, loveless marriage at the centre of his new life becomes strained by his presence he learns that the contemporary American 'good life' is an even more dangerous place for him.[33] In the end, the dog escapes and returns to the streets, chasing cars to ensure his own quick death, dreaming of a heaven where dogs talk and live with the people they love, and ultimately imagining a better world beyond this one.

This pairing of a critique of the immediate social world with an invitation to create and to value a better one signals not so much a new pattern as a recent intensification of this direction in mutt representations. Published the same year as *Timbuktu*, John Berger's novel *King: A Street Story* tells a similar story of homelessness even more directly from a dog's perspective. The novel outlines one momentous day in the life of a community of squatters, described by King, a nondescript dog who elects to live with them. Here the theme of solidarity prevails, since living together clearly mitigates the vulnerability endemic to street life, but it also unequivocally develops distinct canine and human terms of sociality.

Seemingly telepathic, King communicates with these people, and their conversations structure the novel through the course of the day in which their illegal makeshift homes are destroyed. Although unrealistic, the 'magic' of this cross-species language is linked to the construction of identity and reality, depicted as an ongoing process integral to becoming homeless. 'Madness' for the homeless becomes a way of finding stability and, as in Auster's novel, a trope for friction between the real and the fictional. Throughout the story, all the characters describe themselves and each other in flux, never just as they are now but always in contrast to who they were 'before', giving the lie to their own mantra, 'Things are simpler if you take a new name.' Instead, everything including identity is difficult for those who live without steady income, running water, electricity or even guaranteed shelter, and the most difficult thing of all seems to be the most necessary, that is, hanging on to each other. The final collapse of their temporary homes, condemned and bulldozed by the end, puts the necessity of identifying with each other to the test. King, running around the 'wasteland' to lead the people away to safety, imagines each person transformed into a different breed of dog, together forming 'a wild pack',[34] deriving comfort from and freedom in companionship as well as significantly stable canine identities. Predictably, this future proves illusory for the mongrel and his human pack.

Charlie Chaplin and Scraps the dog in a still from Chaplin's film *A Dog's Life* (1918).

A still from Paul Mazursky's 1986 film *Down and Out in Beverly Hills*.

What these novels together suggest is how the construction of an elite group always requires a larger social structure as a foundation, a context in which many more are exploited. Here the dogs are not simply substitutes (metaphors) but more complexly connections (metonyms) to this foundation. An early example of this kind of narrative is Charlie Chaplin's *A Dog's Life* (1918), a film in which the Little Tramp pairs up with a bitch named Scraps, much to their mutual benefit. He saves her from other dogs; she leads him to a fortune; and, like Benji's, their story ends happily off the streets in a new home. In retrospect, this story stakes out an alternate pattern of representing the connections between indigent man and dog as not simply elemental or customary but more profoundly socially conditioned. And towards the end of the century this kind of story proliferated. *Down and Out in Beverly Hills* (the film of 1986 and the short-lived television series of 1987) varies the premise by depicting an owned dog who beseeches a homeless savant to cure the dog's neurotic human family, reconnecting them to each other and to the worlds around them. Although again couched as a comedy, the film parallels these more serious fictions of 'worthless' dogs and humans, together asserting how the values of the ruling classes condition the lives of others customarily excluded from their rarefied worlds.

The conclusions of these fictions echo those of Lars Eighner, whose autobiography of 1993, *Travels with Lizbeth: Three Years on the Road and on the Streets*, provides a straightforward, first-hand account of a homeless man's life with his 'ordinary' mutt Lizbeth. Even more striking in comparison with the history of mongrel representations, Eighner's accounts of life with Lizbeth encapsulate the development of this lesser known tradition. If 'sentiment' keeps him and Lizbeth together at first, then their rapidly worsening conditions through the process of becoming

Lars Eighner and faithful companion Lizbeth, Austin, Texas. 1989.

homeless quickly restructure their intimacy around the desperate work of survival. 'For months at a time' living 'leash-length from each other almost constantly', man and dog subsist – however barely – in Eighner's first-hand stories of abject poverty.[35] But sentiment runs into social critique in the extraordinary process of representing his life with this dog, suggesting how the parallel conditions of homeless people and stray or feral canines enabled a strikingly different pattern of representing dogs to challenge the dominance of breed narratives at the end of the twentieth century.

Through their years together, Eighner writes of his working relationship with Lizbeth as transforming into a mainstay of identity. Living with this spayed mongrel bitch becomes instinctive through a mutual reliance that Eighner describes later in terms of bodily extension:

It was, of course, in urban places that I was happy to have her wake me when people approached us at night. This happened often enough to convince me that I wanted never to be both homeless and dogless. . . . A few experiences like that and I think anyone would have to stop to think if forced to choose between his dog and his own arm. And I am not talking about a Lassie, a fictional dog who knows somehow to go for a doctor in case of illness and for the sheriff in case of criminals. I am talking about a rather ordinary dog doing as any ordinary dog might. To say I trusted Lizbeth in matters within her purview would hardly express it. Do I 'trust' my fingers to hit some key (if not precisely the right one) as I type? After a while I relied on her, without really noticing that I was.[36]

Especially in the contrast between the actual mutt and the fictional collie, the radical separation of homeless gay man and non-breed (and non-breeding) dog from the comforts of the domestic sphere indicates sea changes in attitudes toward dogs and their representation. At one level, this passage documents patterns theorized by the psychologist Kenneth Shapiro in terms of a dog's privileging of spatiality over the human's central value of temporality, as well as how these different ways of looking at the world lead to the dog's focus on immediacy and the human's on history.[37] But, at another level, this passage also clarifies how these developments involve new approaches to dogs as social actors, as not simply aesthetic, sexual and scientific objects but also agents or active participants in these cultural spheres. In declaring that Lizbeth matters not because of what she is but what she does, Eighner models a radically egalitarian sensibility that, like Ackerley's, grounds new possibilities for canine and human identity alike.

Travels with Lizbeth makes this point even more clearly through its subtle relationship with a literary antecedent.

Franz Marc, *Dog in front of the World*, 1912, oil on canvas.

Intermittently tracing their travels across the US Southwest, Eighner's book-length account of his destitute life with Lizbeth interweaves contemporary political commentary and personal narrative and thus shadows a similar book of a previous generation, John Steinbeck's *Travels with Charley, in Search of America* (1962). Both authors write about how sharing their travels with their dogs gives them insight into the most compelling social issues of their times. Steinbeck, describing racism and segregation in the 1960s, feels the hatred directly when for a fleeting moment the back of his standard poodle's head is mistaken for that of a black man in his truck cab. Growing disgusted at the obvious inequities that have become institutional in the US, Steinbeck cuts short his trip and goes home, an option that is not open in the same sense to Eighner. Describing the homeless relationship with his dog in terms of a transference of 'home' as an anchor of identity into her canine body, he highlights his special relationship with his dog: 'For the longest time', Eighner reflects years after Lizbeth's death, 'home was where she was, and I'm sure to her home was where I was'.[38] Not just the relationship but the identities of dog and man are shaped by these circumstances.

Eighner's narrative of this process begins with his decision to quit his job under threat of being fired and discovering that, as an able-bodied, non-breeding single man who has no chemical addictions and has not committed a serious crime, the social services in his native Texas have nothing to offer him. Moreover, he is categorically excluded from homeless shelters because of his decision to keep his mutt Lizbeth rather than relinquish her to an animal shelter, where as a mutt she would probably be not adopted but killed. Although not a breed dog like Charley, Lizbeth is also described as charming, a dog who not only leads the author to positive interactions with strangers but also, in Lizbeth's case, to display an untutored 'talent for hustling' that Eighner incredulously accounts for in terms of 'natural selection'.[39] In both narratives, the occasional acts of human kindness elicited by dogs contrasts starkly with the consistent fear and loathing expressed by privileged people for the disadvantaged, a condition that gives the lie to middle-class illusions about equal rights and justice in America.

But here the comparison ends. Steinbeck, by the time of his story an established literary giant, uses his breed dog as a metaphor for his own aging, for instance, attributing his own prostate problems to his dog.[40] Eighner, whose story ends as he starts to earn money from his writing, outlines a much more complicated relationship with the dog who was initially dumped on him but eventually becomes 'all I had'. While on the street, Eighner lives in constant fear of run-ins with the law not for his own sake but for that of Lizbeth, who as a poorly trained, adult, mixed-breed dog stands little chance of adoption. When she is impounded allegedly for attacking someone, he describes himself as uncharacteristically 'hysterical' at first and then grieving, inconsolable, until through an unlikely series of events he gets the means to free her. The dog cannot know that she is about to be gassed, 'like the prisoners on death row',[41] but the man who thus stands to lose his 'home' does. Here, as with Ackerley, the connection between homosexuality, canine companionship and public space starts to create a more complicated relationship (and ideas about dog–human interrelationships) than the simple metaphorical substitution or appropriation characteristic of *Call of the Wild* and *Stickeen*.

Between Eighner and Lizbeth, a metonymic relationship grows that offers insight into existing as well as potential models of identity and community. Lizbeth, a spayed mutt, shares only some of the same hazards of poverty with her human companion. Where she risks death for displaying aggression, he risks imprisonment and torture for displaying affection in public. A sexually active gay man, Eighner describes himself as poor but sympathetic, always willing to share what little he has with people with AIDS, in part because social services are so clearly discriminatory. But he also documents self-censorship as well; just by contrasting how a heterosexual couple have sex in a public park in broad daylight while he and other gay men more discreetly conduct 'guerrilla workshops on safe sex' in a park restroom, this narrative clarifies how people internalize over-arching cultural prejudices and consequently not simply consent to but more profoundly participate in the daily work of maintaining another's hegemony, the power of a few over them, much to their own detriment.

Jean-Léon Gérôme, *O PTI CIEN* ('O petit chien'), painted shop-sign, 1902, oil on canvas with optical paraphernalia attached to the frame.

The parallel between human sexual orientations and dogs' non-breed or breed status becomes clearer when one examines mutt representations. Lizbeth, had she been a breed member or a product of a human-sanctioned canine sex act, would fare better in the pound, just as Eighner would had he engaged in heterosexual sex and especially fathered children. Together, however, they provide for each other, she through hustling and he through scavenging in 'Dumpsters' (skips). Moreover, something akin to the sense of enrichment experienced by people working with guide dogs appears to grow here, an extension of bodily senses as well as a less tangible sense of belonging. 'Home' thereby becomes not simply transferred into mongrel bodies but transformed by them; mutual reliance leads to an extraordinary relationship with an ordinary dog, which transforms customary structures of identification.

'The Earl of Bridgewater and His Dogs', frontispiece to John Richard Green's *Historical Studies* (1903).

Although considerably more rare than breed-dog representations, images and stories of the mutt have done more than simply contrast or document the average dog's life across the centuries. In their alignment of forms of social oppression especially, the street stories and scenes represent the non-breed dog as part of a mixed community, living with – and not simply alongside – people and other animals. Moving from simply representing oppressed peoples to helping them and others to imagine new forms of identity and society, in the twentieth century especially the mutt gained a significance that was more than mere counterpoint or context to the rise of the breed dog. Instead it was deadlocked with the modern concept of breed. If in one sense, by the mid-nineteenth century, the organization of kennel clubs to maintain stud books and regulate annual dog shows created the breed dog, in another it also opened this process of institutionalization to scrutiny by clarifying how canine (and human) social status was not a 'pure' biological product but a result of combined material, social and symbolic changes.

Through the rise of breed, the public image of the dog more generally moves between poster-child for anti-cruelty causes – including protests of animal fighting, vivisection and hauling – and emblem of bourgeois family life. In the process the non-breed dog increasingly becomes associated with social critique and the breed dog with the status quo. As the earlier discussion of war dogs indicated, this development creates tension within public images of and ideas about dogs. But it also tests the boundaries of representation.

Here the difference between seeing dogs as isolated individuals – the canine 'star' or charismatic breed dog – and as socially connected to humans and other animals through scientific discourses is crucial to understanding this development. The lone canine narrator of Franz Kafka's 'Investigations of a Dog' (1946) concludes with a call for an 'ultimate science',[42] at once reinforcing his overall attempt to speak for all dogs as well as the potential for such representation 'to express another possible community and to forge the means for another consciousness and another sensibility'.[43] For this reason, the final chapter compares the scientific stories and images of dogs that more recently have come to model the future of humans and dogs.

4 Dog Futures

So far this canine cultural history has argued that dogs have shared our central experiences to such a degree that humanity, as the eighteenth-century novelist Horace Walpole suggested, might be better termed 'dogmanity'.[1] Still, most people consider the history of dogs as one of utter dependence on human indulgence. The past two chapters addressed how this contradiction has troubled dog breeders and advocates alike for the past few centuries, but in recent decades it has arguably created even more trouble for scientific practice. Dogs persist within human worlds because of their ready availability and especially their adaptability to extreme conditions, but these qualities also ensure them prominent roles in research, exploration and technological development. In this context, the children's film *Cats and Dogs* (2001), which imagines dogs as worldwide secret-agent-style silent protectors of human scientific invention, appears not so far off the mark. Dogs contributed to some of the most profound scientific breakthroughs of the twentieth century, and they have helped us to learn not only about where we humans have been but also to question where we are heading, in the broadest sense. Particularly through their representation in science fact and fiction, dogs have been the catalysts of significant changes and even profound critiques.

Dogs are the most frequently used companion animals in laboratory research. Their tractability and ready availability make them ideal research subjects, yet these traits also inspire a profound mixture of sentiments. For these reasons, as dogs (and laboratory research more generally) have become more common, their role has become a significant point of contention, at the same time that individual dogs have served as highly visible markers of achievement. Here, too, breeding has proved significant, for each year thousands of dogs – mostly

172

beagles – are 'purpose-bred' as 'lab workers'[2] or experimental research subjects. Ostensibly because the purpose breeding of dogs produces more consistent results (less variation) in research studies, the practice should displace the earlier custom of using strays and unwanted pets for this purpose. Yet the latter method remains appealing to researchers, because such dogs are much cheaper to obtain. This prevalence of dogs, particularly in medical research, makes it all the more surprising that scientists have only recently begun to focus on developing basic knowledge of canine genetics, ecology and reproductive biology.

In another sense, this scientific presence is a reflection of the more widespread cultural significance of dogs. Just as dogs have been necessary to ocean and Arctic exploration, they have proved crucial to the development of space travel. Less predictably, the emerging lab science aesthetic of research subjects produced through 'controlled strains' (carefully documented and limited lines of descent) brought the purity of breed under scrutiny in the twentieth century. Scientific approaches promise to reinvigorate breed, helping breeders to make informed choices so as to obtain the best results, at the same time that they offer the most scathing critique of 'line breeding', especially in terms of the health costs to dogs. The movement towards the use of breed dogs as research subjects further suggests how other kinds of dogs become more threatening in the process. Paralleling the ways in which representations of non-breed and stray dogs especially have been useful tools for cultural critique, such dogs are frequently used in science fiction to give voice to our worst fears, including, in recent years, nuclear holocaust, artificial mutation and biological terrorism. If the mixed history of dogs and humans inspires perpetual conflict among origin myths, their combined contributions towards shaping the future similarly challenge the tales of the modern scientific progress of humanity.

Two extremes of dogs in science in *A Close Shave* (1995) clarify this point. This is the most recent film in the director Nick Park's claymation (stop-action animated) series featuring the bumbling human inventor Wallace and his dog Gromit. Clearly compensating for his master's failings, Gromit never talks, and his significant silences, like those of Bertie Wooster's Jeeves in P. G. Wodehouse's novels, become the stuff of comedy in the earlier films. In *A Close Shave*, however, the stakes are raised, since Gromit's silence enables him to be framed for sheep rustling. Part murder mystery, part *Frankenstein*, the film enriches Gromit's role as co-inventor, lab technician and troubleshooting genius by pitting him against a 'cyberdog', whose equally multifaceted but evil genius includes not only setting up Gromit to take his rustling rap but also industrial slaughtering, thieving intellectual property and threatening the mistress he was invented to protect. At face value, the two dogs seem to add new twists to old canine dichotomies – natural / cultural, wild / tame, dominating / dominated – but the story undermines such simple oppositions. The cyberdog is overcome only by the combined efforts of sheep, dog and man; the idea along with the embodiment of dog created by man becomes overwhelmed (literally crushed) by these more complex cross-species configurations. Envisioning dogs as actively involved in creating and controlling (even themselves as) experimental research, the film subtly offers insight into the contradictory assumptions about dogs in science and their influential changes in the twentieth century.

In part because dogs have been notoriously difficult to categorize, *Canis familiaris* was largely neglected in the eighteenth and nineteenth century except as an instrument in research, particularly vivisection. Through incidents like the Brown Dog Riots, however, such dogs gained social visibility as the victims of scientific excess. Given this prominence, dogs understandably inspired crucial contributions to the critique of positivism, the faith in pure objectivity or reason and facts removed from social influence that prevailed among late nineteenth- and early twentieth-century researchers. At stake here was not only the character of scientific enquiry but also the idea of science as 'advancing' humanity, seen thus as both a discrete entity and an end in itself.

One of the earliest internal challenges to this viewpoint shows how the relationships of dogs with people challenge the core faith in objectivity. Proposing an innovative concept of 'animal sociology', in 1928 Read Bain lamented that science 'sadly neglected' what literature made abundantly obvious: although 'Darwin, with his customary keenness, described the similarities and interdependence of dogs and men in the expression of emotion', subsequent scientists ignored it and instead developed biological models of culture by focusing exclusively on other animals, such as social insects and primates.[3] Such neglect not only compromised scientific objectivity but also revealed a more troubling concern, namely an aversion to questioning how scientists achieve this ideal position.

The omnipresence of dogs across human histories and cultures highlights the impossibility of such transcendence. Like labour without alienation, humans are almost unthinkable without dogs and, while Karl Marx in *Capital* (1867) uses Daniel Defoe's novel *Robinson Crusoe* (1719) as an exception that proves the rule of alienated labour, even Crusoe had a dog. Achieving scientific objectivity is tantamount to ignoring the dogs, and to underscore the problems that this creates, particularly for sociology, Bain's article ends with the likewise exceptional example of 'white dogs', trained by white people to attack black people, specifically asking whether such dogs exhibit 'canine race prejudice'.[4] Even now, the acknowledgement (let alone an interpretation of the significance of) this phenomenon remains highly controversial – the film adaptation of 1982 of Romain Gary's novel *White Dog* proved so troubling that it was suppressed by studio executives and never released theatrically in the US – in part because such dogs pinpointed the central problem for science of how to apply biological absolutes such as species boundaries to constantly shifting social contexts.

The avoidance of questions of how dogs become actors in human social networks makes it easier to use dogs in experimental research, but, especially since this approach became the norm, it also dramatically increased the profile of studies that addressed these questions directly. Forty years after Bain challenged scientists to take dogs seriously, J. P. Scott and J. L. Fuller's ground-breaking study, *Genetics and the Social Behavior of Dogs*, began with a similar admission that 'the dog, for all its eight thousand years or so of association with human beings' was 'still in many respects a scientifically unknown animal'.[5] Scott and Fuller did much to reverse this trend by tracing several generations of breed and hybrid dogs in a laboratory setting. Their book condenses more than 50 years of research on the domestic dog at the Jackson Laboratory in Bar Harbor, Maine, and has been influential in developing conceptions of human behaviour, for instance, that infantile experiences are the most important in shaping adult behavioural patterns, and that 'smart' individuals are not born but socially conditioned.[6]

In addition to posing a profound challenge to eugenicist stereotypes of genetic research, the book shows how the dog is of paramount interests to research on humans. Offering much by way of practical genetic advice for the dog breeder, Scott

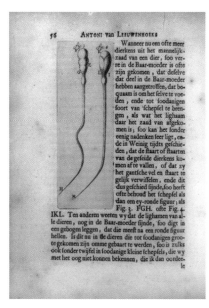

Wanneer nu een ofte meer dierkens uit het mannelijk-zaad van een dier, foo ver-re in de Baar-moeder is ofte zijn gekomen, dat defelve dat deel in de Baar-moeder hebben aangetroffen, dat bo-quaam is om het felve te voe-den, ende tot foodanigen foort van fchepfel te bren-gen, als wat het lighaam daar het zaad van afgeko-men is; foo kan het fonder eenig nadenken feer ligt, en-de in Weinig tijdts gefchie-den, dat de ftaart of ftaarten van de gefeide dierkens ko-men af te vallen, of dat zy het gantfche vel en ftaart te gelijk verwiffelen, ende dit dus gefchied fijnde, foo heeft ofte behoud het fchepfel als dan een ey-ronde figuur, als Fig. 3. ofte Fig. 4. IKL. Ten anderen weeten wy dat de lighamen van al-le dieren, nog in de Baar-moeder fijnde, foo digt in een gebogen leggen, dat die meeft na een ronde figuur hellen. Is dit nu in de dieren die tot foodanigen groo-te gekomen zijn onmte gebaart te werden, foo is zulks ook fonder twijfel in foodanige kleine fchepfels, die wy met het oog niet konnen bekennen, die ik dan oordee-le

Living and dead spermatozoa from a dog as seen through a microscope, an engraved illustration from Anthony van Leeuwenhoek's *Ontledingen en ontdekkingen* (Leiden, 1696–1718).

and Fuller ultimately argue that, because dogs have been cohabitating with humans for thousands of years yet have reproduced so much more rapidly (in generations of two as opposed to our twenty years), 'the dog may be a genetic pilot experiment for the human race'.[7] As the animal companions that have shared most directly and continuously the cultural and environmental pressures that have shaped human soci-eties, dogs can help us to predict and otherwise troubleshoot the genetic consequences for humans of settled life. With this theory they appeal both to genetic scientists to take research on dogs more seriously and extend the ecological redefinitions of dogs as central to humanity.

More broadly, this shifting ecological sensibility led to the methodological development of the field study in the twentieth

century, but here too research on dogs remains under-repre-
sented. Ten years after Scott and Fuller, Alan Beck addressed
the disparity between the few field studies of feral dogs and
'more than a million laboratory studies using dogs'[8] with *The
Ecology of Stray Dogs: A Study of Free-Ranging Urban Animals.*
Focusing on Baltimore as a typical US city in the early 1970s,
Beck affirms his central hypothesis – that man and dog are very
much a part of each other's ecology – by observing canine and
human interactions in the city. Roving, abandoned and lost pets
sustain the overall stray-dog population in partnership with
humans, who feed all of these dogs through handouts and
rubbish to their mutual peril. Such 'free-ranging' dogs prove
far more likely than restrained dogs to bite people and to die
young, mostly killed by cars and disease.

The public health implications especially fuelled rapid shifts
in popular conceptions of the responsibilities of dog ownership,
as well as community management of stray populations. Beck
emphasized the serious risks that free-ranging dogs pose as
carriers of at least 65 diseases in humans, including those linked
to parasites and 'cross invaders' (a kind of disease that afflicts
each species in different ways, such as the one that appears as
measles in humans and distemper in dogs).[9] Many are spread
by direct contact with dogs as well as with their faeces, which
also contaminate water supplies. Dramatically increased public
spending on animal control, subsidized spay / neuter programmes and the enforcement of leash laws have all proceeded
from this and subsequent research on free-ranging dogs.
More subtly, in the US unrestrained dogs are no longer socially
acceptable. Barbara Bush's dog books are indications of this,
since they describe her free-ranging dog routinely overturning
the neighbours' rubbish bins in the 1970s,[10] while in the 1980s
her next dog was strictly fenced in.

The most direct and obvious changes concern public attitudes toward dog faeces as 'litter'[11] that led quickly to the adoption and enforcement of poop-scoop laws in many major cities across the world. This change in attitude towards dog shit directly affects human relationships with dogs, adding responsibility and expense to pet keeping and along the way enhancing its cultural meanings. For dog faeces, the glaring exception to the psychoanalyst Sigmund Freud's rule of excrement abhorrence, 'permit us to bring the whole act of defecation into social space' and therefore provide people in modern industrial societies with 'the only acceptable way to represent shit'.[12] The chow-dog breeder Freud's passion for his pet dogs, unchecked even when working (according to the poet and analysand H.D.), may have led to this blind spot in his theory. Even as early as the seventeenth century, Rembrandt's image of the Good Samaritan suggests that dog shit is more than simply a fact of urban life. Whether as a sign of randomness or a mechanism for social deviance – exemplified in another unforgettable image of Baltimore, the culminating sequence of the cult film *Pink Flamingos* (1972), in which the transvestite Divine demonstrates that she is 'the Most Disgusting Person in the World' by eating dog shit – this potentially toxic organic substance is also a highly charged cultural artefact. Public ordinances that now require dog walkers to remove it from public property therefore not only promote hygiene but also measure a dramatic alteration in the relationships among dogs and humans.

As the primary object of daily dog walks, it more subtly contributes to the theoretical development of more viable scientific values, a crucial turning point in the interrogation of pure objectivity. Donna Haraway, a feminist historian of science, was inspired by walking her dogs to develop the concept of scientific observation in terms of 'situated knowledges' as an alternative

Mark Hughes's cartoon drawn for the Love the Lake / Scoop the Poop Campaign.

A street sign in Portland, Maine, in 2003.

to the 'god trick' (purely detached objectivity).[13] Haraway imagines seeing the world that she and her dogs encounter every day through their eyes; the different human / canine biological mechanisms lead to different relative perceptions and consequently different understandings (situated knowledges) of the same phenomena, a variety of viewpoints that her dogs help her to see as mutually enhancing rather than negating each other or vying for dominance. Science becomes all the more clearly a set of social phenomena, the goals of which are more readily achieved when multiple perspectives (including those of other species) are valued. Just as dogs highlight what is at stake in distinguishing nature from culture (exemplifying the difficulty of defining species), dogs clarify the complex relations between culture and science (clarifying how even scientific knowledge is embodied).

Consequently, the current redefinition of dog shit as litter is not simply 'good science' but reflective of larger cultural shifts towards valuing Western scientific knowledge over other traditional ways of knowing the world. Across cultures and for millennia, dog shit was considered medicine among humans and a variety of things for dogs, who eat it and communicate by scent. It continues to be a way of learning about each other (if not more literally getting a taste of someone else's life). Haraway makes this point explicitly as she describes how cleaning up after her dogs not only makes her a good citizen but also becomes an opportunity to critique the cultural effects of technology and science:

As I glove my hand in the plastic film – courtesy of the research empires of industrial chemistry – that protects my morning *New York Times* to pick up the microcosmic ecosystems, called scat, produced anew each day by my

> dogs, I find pooper scoopers quite a joke, one that lands me back in the histories of the incarnation, political economy, technoscience, and biology.[14]

Dog shit figures the social and messily embodied relationships of science across species lines. And, by amplifying the echo of 'species' in 'specie' ('filthy lucre' as 'the join in Marx and Freud'), Haraway uses this typical image of its lawful removal to figure the redefinition of cross-species relationships within 'modern US dog culture' and modern industrial societies more generally.

But growing awareness of this ecological complexity also muddles efforts to distinguish the special significance of dogs to humans. Studies of canine reproductive biology make this particularly apparent, for potentially they produce a better understanding of the unique physiology of dogs at the same time as they offer to regulate and thereby strengthen the exploitative commercial structures of breed. *The Missyplicity Project*, the official website of the most prominent dog-cloning study, amplifies these problems. The site exhibits many unique and socially progressive aspects of this particular project: its scientifically unique focus on cloning a random-bred animal, a mutt named Missy; its ethical commitment to the placement of all dogs involved in the project, pioneering a model that could minimize the staggering numbers of dogs routinely killed at the end of such studies; and the consistently public presentation of its work through the site itself. But its constant appeal to the sentimental rhetorics of breed more clearly contradicts the central assumption that dog cloning promises to improve the lives of such mutts, let alone preserve presently endangered wild canids.[15] Like dog breeders, the developers of the project have clear commercial incentives as well; along with the first successful cat-cloning project, it is now underwritten by

Genetic Savings & Clone, a gene bank that plans to offer commercial pet-cloning services. The direct appeal to people mourning the loss of a pet dog – the premise of the futuristic nightmare of human cloning in the film of 2000, *The 6th Day* – may still seem the stuff of science fiction, but its primary vehicle, the mutt at the centre of *Missyplicity*, illustrates a more familiar use of high-profile dogs in the results of scientific research to deflect questions about methods and objectives.

No dog represents this process better than Laika, a former stray selected by scientists in the Soviet Union to become the first mammal to travel successfully to outer space. Dogs were the focus of Russian biomedical research up to that point because of the early success of Ivan Pavlov,[16] who during what became his Nobel prize-winning research on saliva and the digestive tract began to notice the association between pre-feeding rituals and the salivation of the dogs who were his research subjects. As part of identifying the 'freedom reflex', Pavlov conducted experiments from 1889 until his death in 1936 that included inducing neurosis in tractable dogs,[17] in other words, torturing the dogs selected precisely for their trusting character to prove that insanity can be artificially created.[18] International acclaim for this work ensured that the dog would continue to be a research animal of choice among Soviet scientists.

Like Pavlov's dogs, Laika was specifically selected and punished for her willingness to be trained; while she made history as she entered space in the orbiting satellite Sputnik II on 3 November 1957, no provisions were made for the return of the dog who had led man into space,[19] and she was to die of severe trauma a few hours after the mission started. Her achievement nonetheless proved an important propaganda tool in the Cold War Space Race; the US president, John Kennedy, was outraged by such a glaring example of Soviet technological superiority

Laika strapped in the Sputnik II seat, 1957.

and, presumably to rub salt into his wounds, was later sent a puppy from Strelka, one of the dogs who had successfully returned from the next mission. But Laika's legacy includes the lie that she enjoyed a few days orbiting the earth in her capsule. Only after 40 years had passed did researchers admit that they had deliberately deceived the public into thinking that she 'lived to see the 40th anniversary of the October Revolution and then died peacefully'.[20] Like Pavlov's dogs, she was later honoured with a monument at the biomedical research centre where she underwent testing,[21] a backhanded compliment that reinforces the customary scientific role of dogs as sacrificial objects and silent servants.

This manufacture of canine scientific heroism surreptitiously involves a mixture of guilt and disdain that becomes all the more perverse as the dogs' sufferings become silenced, justified as a means of minimizing those of others. Another mutt hero named Anna, the only animal whose portrait hangs in the Johns Hopkins Medical Research Library, was the first successfully to be surgically altered to mimic a human heart defect, and then to be 'repaired' or re-altered to demonstrate the efficacy of a specific surgical technique. Public and professional prejudices inform this singular memorial. At the height of racial segregation, the mutt herself appeared in promotional newsreels, instead of the inter-racial team of scientists leading the research. But a 2002 documentary reasserted the scientific attitude towards dogs in research by dismissing as it describes Anna's contribution to a means by which medical doctors 'solved the technical problem' of curing the human disorder.[22]

Unequivocal materializations of this prejudice, other surgical techniques have been developed more specifically to silence dogs. One example is 'ventriculochordectomy', a procedure performed on laboratory animals that destroys the vocal chords. To insiders, it is a 'simple' way of preventing a 'nuisance' to lab workers and other animals,[23] but from the outside it looks more like a dovetailing of material practice and symbolic values, rendering dogs unable to vocalize their suffering and enabling human lab workers to ignore it.[24] If the Brown Dog

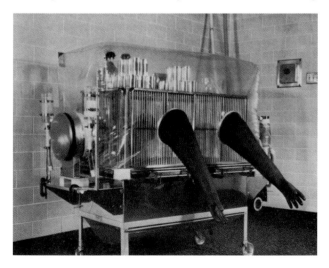

A barrier chamber for SPF (specific-pathogen-free or barrier raised) dogs.

Riots earlier suggested how the familiarity of dogs makes them particularly vexed research tools in the public eye, then these canine vivisections show how dogs become desirable objects of scientific study only after their 'problems' are solved. This mixed legacy of actual dogs in scientific developments also informs the ability of their fictional counterparts to project and to critique these developments. Ten years before the Brown Dog Riots, H. G. Wells projected a similar situation with 'a wretched dog, flayed and otherwise mutilated', who escaped from Dr Moreau's laboratory in London and galvanized public outcry; the dog's cries are heard in the broadest sense and become the narrative premise for the doctor's exile to his infamous island.[25] Long before procedures like ventriculochordectomy became common, canine communication was seen as a dangerous thing for science.

Another fictional account of scientific creation involving dogs clarifies how the ideal research dog is a silent servant. Mikhail Bulgakov's novel of 1925, *Heart of a Dog*, focuses on Sharik, a homeless cur who, like Laika, is captured on the street and, like Anna, is subsequently made the focus of a cutting-edge surgical experiment, in this case the implantation of human body parts that turn the dog temporarily into a man. While the story echoes specifically folk tales of such transformations,[26] it focuses on how xenotransplantation (the exchange of body parts across species lines) fails to fulfil the eugenic promises of biological uplift through science. Seen as symbolic of the average citizen, the story of Sharik, tormented before, during and after the surgeries, exemplifies the broader failings of the Soviet experiment. So threatening was this metaphorical indictment of the political consequences of scientific authoritarianism that the novel was not published in the Soviet Union until 1987.[27] Read literally, the movements of the miserable doglike man /

manlike dog created through science and rejected by society illustrate an even more pervasive problem of the faith in science and technology to solve social problems. In the end, social perceptions, particularly of the dog's ability to speak, are decisive in diagnosing this broader failure; along with his citizenship papers validating his claim to be human, Sharik's new-found ability to make this claim verbally 'does not yet mean being a man'.[28] This silencing of the dog, both in text and context, paradoxically communicates these critical perspectives on the rising social power of scientific discourses all the more effectively.

As Missyplicity suggests, other canine versions of *Frankenstein* invoke breed to redeem the monstrosity of the creators as well as that of their canine creations. Softening the critique of scientific hubris, Tim Burton's short film *Frankenweenie* (1986) imagines the canine creature as a dead pit-bull pet reanimated by his boy owner. Persecuted to a fiery second death (a send-up of James Whale's film version of 1931, not Mary Shelley's novel), Frankenweenie is reanimated yet again along with the neighbour's poodle bitch (replete with the white-streaked frizzy hairdo of Whale's *Bride of Frankenstein* of 1935), this time becoming a means by which his creator eventually wins acceptance from their community for his monstrous dog creations. These dogs never talk, so again the figure of the silent servant prevails, but these uses of breed dogs convey certain messages. A convergence of cultural associations (pit bull as 'killer dog') and gender expectations (poodle as 'bride') proscribes these breed choices, and they also intimate that the non-breed dog is most monstrous of all.

This notion comes to the fore in Kirsten Bakis's novel of 1997, *The Lives of the Monster Dogs*, which features breed dogs who have been implanted with robotic, human-like hands and voices. Here the 'cyberdogs' speak, even reflecting on the

From Tim Burton's 1984 film *Frankenweenie*.

individual and social effects of their transformation, but only when they are breed dogs aspiring to become human. And such communication works to reinforce the ideology of breed. Throughout, the story of the lone mongrel monster dog is told second-hand; this mutt, who inspires the breed members to destroy their human masters and start their own free society, is later killed by them for trying to force himself on a breed bitch. After the mutt monster dies, the breed monsters find that they too cannot govern themselves, that they must either go insane or return to human servitude. As with Poncelet's aristochiens, these creatures gently mock a system that they both reflect and support; breed imposes an all too familiar order even amid the chaotic breakdown of species boundaries. These old notions of dogs as created by and for the service of mankind find new audiences in science fiction and, in the case of Missy's clones (should they ever appear), markets for new techno-scientific products.

More critical perspectives open up in stories that develop the broader social repercussions of such profound changes to humans and dogs, particularly narratives that focus on them as inadvertent by-products of broader scientific endeavours. Harlan Ellison's short story 'A Boy and his Dog' (1970), imagines the evolution of canine-human telepathy as an indirect result of worldwide nuclear war. In the story and its cult film version (1974), this kind of communication in one sense seems an extreme reversion to fantasized evolutionary origins: dogs, unable to locate or open canned food, have to rely on free-ranging human scavengers, and in return provide them with

From L. Q. Jones's 1975 film *A Boy and his Dog*.

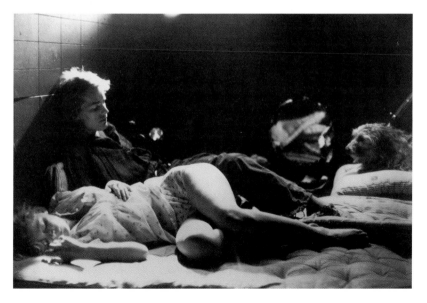

189

advance warning of others. This hostile and toxic context deepens the title characters' sense of interdependence, since cross-species telepathy serves much more than these basic needs. The title dog Blood also teaches history to his boy, Vic, providing him with the perspective needed to understand his past and to make decisions that will ensure their future. Reinforcing this complexity, the story explicitly rejects not only the certainty of scientific uplift but also the fantasy that people alone will prevail through nuclear holocausts. In the end Vic flees the underground remnants of human civilization, electing instead to hunt these people in the radioactive wastelands with Blood, enabling Ellison to spin two more stories, illustrated with the original as the graphic novel of 2003, *Vic and Blood: The Continuing Adventures of a Boy and his Dog*. No longer simply disposable instruments or silent servants in the advancement of human knowledge, dogs in this sci-fi vision of the future continue to help to define as well as to negotiate social boundaries.

In futuristic stories, however, dogs also reinforce the threats involved when these barriers break down. Bio-terroristic threats perhaps provide the most immediate context for interrogating this potential. While misanthropic or sloppy scientists typically take this role in the popular imagination, in Richard Adams's novel of 1977, *The Plague Dogs*, escaped laboratory dogs are cast as potential vectors of biological weapons, in this case experimental bubonic plague. Here again the dog as research subject is a catalyst of a broader critique of the monstrous excesses of socially isolated human scientists. The title dogs, Rowf and Snitter, are a former stray mutt and a former pet fox terrier; in these ways they represent the bulk of the millions of dogs who have been used in research science. Atypically, they liberate themselves from torturous experiments, including multiple near-drownings for the one and repeated brain surgeries for the other, in a secret government laboratory, and in the process of their escape wander into its bubonic plague testing facility.

Told primarily from the animals' point of view, the novel explores how and why the dogs become feral yet remain dependent on humans. As public knowledge of the potential plague contamination spreads, they become 'plague dogs' in the popular imagination, not only imagined transmitters of a deadly disease but, perhaps more importantly to humans, the focus of a sensational nationwide media campaign. Reviled by people and faced with starvation and death from exposure, the dogs argue over whether life with humans ever can be equitable for dogs. These discussions become all the more poignant as the 'plague' the dogs release turns out to be not a biological but a social disease. While the dark ending of the animated film version of 1982 affirms the idea that humans are a social and scientific menace to dogs, the novel clarifies how scientists along with politicians and reporters squabble with each other in order to use dogs to fulfil their own desires. Taken together, the dogs of these texts clearly communicate how the development of biological, nuclear and other large-scale tools of destruction always involves mass deception.

Current international politics make this point even more compelling. Central figures of human identification, dogs are embraced more favourably by some countries, especially when people use them to represent themselves.[29] In this way, for instance, J.R.R. Tolkien's identification of his science-fantasy dog Roverandom as 'an English' dog can be seen as endearing,[30] not just biographical.[31] While war-dog histories tend to focus on these positive identifications, dogs in science fact and fiction have been used in a variety of ways to promote and extend wars that are being waged all over the world today.

A scene from
Martin Rosen's
film *The Plague
Dogs.*, first
released in 1982,
in Germany.

In 2002, videotaped images of rudimentary experiments
(allegedly al-Qaeda images of the former Darunta camp in
Afghanistan) were obtained by CNN, which touted one contain-
ing images of dogs left to die in rooms filling with toxic vapours
as 'possibly the saddest and scariest tape of all'.[32] Although this
type of gas poisoning is among the many methods recommend-
ed by the US government for euthanizing laboratory dogs,[33]
these everyday plague dogs are usually kept out of the public
eye. The commentary clarifies how this exceptional introduction
of the images to a public forum concerns not the representation
of dogs but the manufacture of the ideas of enemies not only as
rogue scientists but also 'puppy' killers.[34] By enabling these

combinations of sentiment and science, old stories and new characters, dogs prove powerful metaphors in international politics. Moreover, their ability to trigger imaginative leaps back and forth between reality and representation – in this case, dogs who were research subjects are videotaped as part of one war, then their representations are broadcast as part of a media campaign that links other wars – make them indispensable to constructing present and modelling future human societies.

And they do so not only when depicted as victim but also when they are equated with enemies. In Steve Benson's cartoon depicting US–Iraq relations, which specifically addresses the issue of UN weapons inspections, the joke is a familiar story of US capriciousness in foreign policy. And it depends on a related narrative of American imperialism, a relationship here depicted

Steve Benson, 'Saddam, sit!', cartoon in the *Maine Sunday Telegram* (5 January 2003).

as an inept or cruel trainer to others, who are grovelling, subservient dogs. Ridiculed by the comic, this kind of story, which represents the enemy as 'a veritable fiend, less worthy of compassion than a mad dog',[35] also has an ancient history as a method of discriminating against whole groups of other people. Representing others as doglike and therefore 'sub-human'[36] works as well for internal critique, identifying only to deride the doggy ways of people within your group. This kind of dog images loomed large in popular protests throughout the world in 2003, especially in Britain and Australia, where the prime ministers were depicted in effigy as dogs on leashes led by the smiling, human-like effigies of President George W. Bush.

In the broader historical context, the image of Saddam Hussein as a dog to Bush's master also indicates a sea change in perceptions of Iraq's relationship to the world. More than a decade ago, a very different pattern of animal imaging in the US figured Iraq as a more localized threat[37] to secure a regional, Middle Eastern and Arab cultural identity that connects Hussein directly to a story of Iraq as a regional threat (to justify war after the invasion of Kuwait). In the UK at that time, the shift toward describing this leader as a 'wild dog' and later a 'mad dog'[38] offered a foretaste of how such associations ten years later would not simply reinforce cultural difference but more compellingly present his leadership as a global threat. Whether laughably literal or menacingly monstrous, such depictions necessarily overwrite the political and economic specificity of modern international relations with thousand-years-old cultural associations. For the dog is after all the animal that now most visibly inhabits the whole world along with the human. For better and worse, the history of dogs has become inextricable from that of humans. From the dogs of the war gods in the ancient world through the proverbial British bulldogs and German war dogs of more recent centuries, images and stories become a way of making sense of conflicts between and within human societies. Promoted through these dog images, such associations helped to motivate hundreds of thousands of people in 2003 to go to and to protest against war.

But this process has also involved the suppression of other images and stories of human-canine interactions. During the Gulf War of 1991, reporters from ITV filmed free-ranging dogs feeding on the corpses of dead Iraqi people, 'just for the record'.[39] A fate reserved for the worst offenders in ancient stories, including the biblical Jezebel and Oedipus' son (and Antigone's brother) Polyneices, the concept of humans as dog meat has become perhaps even more offensive (certainly more sensational) in the industrialized world; ITV archived but never broadcast these taboo scenes. Images of people abandoned in death by their own society, contemptuously ignored by enemy forces and consumed by dogs as foodstuffs attest to the inevitability of degradation and deprivation in war. Not simply withheld but more complexly supplanted by the hybrid human-canine images of political leaders, these dogs and people together become at once spectres of the past and future.

This book thus ends where it began with the ubiquity of the dog and of our mixed feelings about it. The creatures powerful enough to be man's best friends also feed our deepest fears and prejudices. Representations that appeal to prevalent notions of the dog as a despised and degraded human make subtle feelings of prejudice toward other people visible and immediate. But no less meaningful is their ability, through depictions as noble animals, to deepen awareness of empathy and to inspire extensions of sympathy for others. The convergence of these conflicting ideas of the dog suggests how, even when individual images ostensibly serve immediate political or social desires,

Saddam Hussein as a dangerous dog, illustration by Alfred Wood in the *Maine Sunday Telegram* (10 November 2002).

they become enmeshed in an ancient and all-too-human struggle to figure our shared histories and destinies.

Whether treated as privileged and personified animal or despised and degraded human,[40] the dog has become an ordinary and mundane species through an extraordinary interface of the histories of canine and human species. Preceding the domestication of other animal species by at least thousands of years,

Edouard Manet, *Tama, the Japanese Dog, c.* 1875, oil on canvas.

dogs have continued to work in cooperation with humans to change the nature of sociality itself ever since. In myth our guides to forbidden zones, our protectors, even our ancestors, dogs remain critical compatriots in the history of human society everywhere. But their participation in constructing our worlds has not always been appreciated. As human rights and social justice movements have brought human classifications of each other under widespread scrutiny, hierarchical categorizations of animals to a lesser degree have also come into question.

Especially in Western scientific cultures, dogs are on the front lines of these struggles, moving from 'separate but equal' status to an integral part of our biological, legal and more profoundly cultural conceptions of who we are.[41] In recent years the medical and especially genetic significance of human-canine proximities has gained interest, leading scientists, for instance, to prioritize drafting the dog genome over those of dolphins, whales and elephants. What is more, people are beginning to understand how not one but two species – theirs and ours – became 'companion' to each other in the process.[42] Neither simply a human creation through domestication nor a tamed wild animal, the dog emerges from such configurations in the space between nature and culture, signalling even as it maintains such cross-species interplay.

The tremendous interest in dogs, which has surged in recent years, has created a wealth of new ways of conceptualizing these relationships, from practical breeding and training methods to more abstract representational questions raised by artists, scientists, historians and museum curators, to name a few. Reprints and digitalization of old dog texts complement this rapid production and widespread dissemination of new materials. While the ready availability of old and new dog materials – including literature, visual art, memoirs, manuals, breeding charts and even the 'barking dog' music genre – may indicate a passing fad, their large and varied audiences suggest that this proliferation is symptomatic of larger political and economic developments.

Either way, these developments affirm humans' long-term interest in dogs in a world in which species difference seems less and less certain. By comparing some of the old representations of dogs and people with the new throughout, this book likewise can only continue what has become a long process of questioning how past ideas have shaped our present ways of seeing dogs. Given the long history, even prehistory, of our cohabitation, taking these questions seriously may enable us to ensure a shared future for canine, human and other species alike.

Timeline of the Dog

c. 50–60,000,000 BC	*c.* 500,000 BC	*c.* 12,000 BC	*c.* 850 BC
Canids first appear in the fossil records and possibly begin to diverge from other carnivore families	Some genetic evidence suggests that *canis familiaris* emerges as a distinct species from *canis lupus*	Archaeological sites in Palestine show humans interred with dogs in stone-covered tombs	Homer composes the Greek epic poem *The Odyssey*. It depicts the hero's dog, Argus, as a realistic and sympatheti character, whose death adds pathos to the end

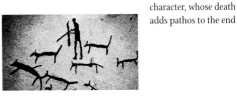

c. 1700–1800	1752	1800–05	1814
Chinese imperial 'dog-book' paintings create a rudimentary record of breed members, and also provide visual standards for Pekinese dogs	Jean-Baptiste Oudry paints *Bitch Hound Nursing her Puppies*, the first of a popular genre of animal mothers, which is an instant critical and popular success	Sydenham Edwards publishes *Cynographia Britannica*, the first of what becomes a prolific type of dog book. It features realistic colour illustrations of dogs and describes them through anecdotes as well as natural history	*Le Chien de Montar* opens in Paris and becomes the water mark of a vogue fo dog dramas

1898–9	1918	1938	1957
Francis Barraud sells *His Master's Voice*, in which a terrier mourns the artist's dead brother, to RCA. The dog becomes a mascot of the corporation	Corporal Lee Duncan finds the German shepherd puppy Rin Tin Tin in a bombed-out kennel in Lorraine. The dog later becomes a film celebrity in the US	The breed dog becomes an international icon through Eric Knight's story 'Lassie Come Home'. Lassie is later turned into a popular film and television character	On 3 November the Sov dog Laika makes histor entering outer space in Sputnik II. She dies of s trauma a few hours afte mission starts

c. 800 BC	*c.* 200 BC–AD 200	*c.* AD 945	1570
Earliest taxonomy of dogs included in the so-called Chinese *Book of Rites*. It offers three vague categories (hunting, guarding and edible), with no mention of pets	Hindi epic *Mahābhārata* ends with a story of redemption through a faithful dog, who then reveals himself as the God of Compassion	The Laws of Wales codified by King Hywel Dda (Hywel the Good) include the world's first detailed classification system of dogs	Johannes Caius, an English royal physician, publishes *De canibus Britannicus*, the first book devoted exclusively to dogs. A popular translation, *Of English Dogges*, appears in 1576

1820s	1836–7	1859	1874
The first live dog takes the role of Dog Toby and becomes a stock feature of the traditional British Punch and Judy puppet theatre	Serial publication of Frederick Marryat's *Snarleyyow; or, The Dog Fiend*, the first novel explicitly to feature a non-breed dog as a major dramatic character	The first event advertised as a dog show held at Newcastle upon Tyne	Publication of the British *Kennel Club Stud Book* initiates formal registration and pedigrees for most breeds. The *American Kennel Club Stud Book* follows in 1878

1965	1973	1997	2003
Publication of *Genetics and the Social Behavior of Dogs*, which argues that dogs are a 'genetic pilot experiment' for the human race	Alan Beck publishes *The Ecology of Stray Dogs: A Study of Free-Ranging Urban Animals*, a ground-breaking field study of canine and human interactions in the city	Foundation of the Missyplicity Project, the first large-scale research project to focus on cloning a non-breed animal, a random-bred former stray named Missy	The dog becomes the latest animal to have its genome sequenced, as Craig Venter completes a genome map of his standard poodle Shadow

References

1 CANINE BEGINNINGS

1 Juliet Clutton-Brock, 'Origins of the Dog: Domestication and Early History', in *The Domestic Dog: Its Evolution, Behaviour and Interactions with People*, ed. James Serpell (Cambridge, 1995), p. 8.

2 Konrad Lorenz, *Man Meets Dog*, trans. Marjorie Kerr Wilson (Harmondsworth, 1964), p. 76.

3 James Serpell, 'The Hair of the Dog', in *The Domestic Dog*, p. 262.

4 Stephen Budiansky, *The Truth about Dogs: An Inquiry into the Ancestry, Social Conventions, Mental Habits and Moral Fiber of Canis familiaris* (New York, 2000), p. 16.

5 Janice Koler-Matznick, 'The Origin of the Dog Revisited', *Anthrozoös*, XV/2 (2002), p. 109.

6 Raymond Coppinger and Richard Schneider, 'Evolution of Working Dogs', in *The Domestic Dog*, p. 33.

7 Koler-Matznick, 'The Origin of the Dog Revisited', p. 110.

8 Clutton-Brock, 'Origins of the Dog', p. 8.

9 Coppinger and Schneider, 'Evolution of Working Dogs', p. 33.

10 Jeffrey Moussaieff Masson, *Dogs Never Lie About Love: Reflections on the Emotional World of Dogs* (New York, 1998), p. 143.

11 Raymond Coppinger and Lorna Coppinger, *Dogs: A New Understanding of Canine Origin, Behavior and Evolution* (Chicago, IL, 2001), pp. 277–81.

12 Lawrence K. Corbett, *The Dingo in Australia and Asia* (Ithaca, NY, 1995), pp. 163–9; see also Coppinger and Coppinger, *Dogs*,

pp. 279–80.

13 Clutton-Brock, 'Origins of the Dog', pp. 10–12.

14 Sophia Menache, 'Dogs and Human Beings: A Story of
    Friendship', *Society & Animals*, vi/1 (1998),
    http://www.psyeta.org/sa/sa6.1/menache.html.

15 Clutton-Brock, 'Origins of the Dog', p. 16.

16 Koler-Matznick, 'The Origin of the Dog Revisited', p. 110; see also
    Marion Schwartz, *A History of Dogs in the Early Americas* (New
    Haven, ct, 1997), p. 18.

17 Coppinger and Schneider, 'Evolution of Working Dogs',
    p. 33; see also Clutton-Brock, 'Origins of the Dog', p. 10.

18 James Serpell, *In the Company of Animals: A Study of
    Human–Animal Relationships* (Cambridge, 1996), p. 45.

19 Clutton-Brock, 'Origins of the Dog', p. 15.

20 Serpell, Introduction, in *The Domestic Dog*, p. 2.

21 C. Fred Bush, *C. Fred's Story*, ed. Barbara Bush (Garden City, ny,
    1984), p. 16.

22 Masson, *Dogs Never Lie*, p. 77.

23 Koler-Matznick, 'The Origin of the Dog Revisited', p. 102.

24 Masson, *Dogs Never Lie*, p. 7.

25 Clutton-Brock, 'Origins of the Dog', p. 9.

26 Koler-Matznick, 'The Origin of the Dog Revisited', p. 109.

27 Coppinger and Schneider, 'Evolution of Working Dogs', p. 35.

28 Lorenz, *Man Meets Dog*, p. 23.

29 Vicki Hearne, *Adam's Task: Calling Animals by Name* (New York,
    1986), p. 22.

30 Koler-Matznick, 'The Origin of the Dog Revisited', p. 107; see also
    Clutton-Brock, 'Origins', pp. 15–26, where it is surmised that the
    earliest colour of dogs' coats was 'tawny', and one of their first dis-
    tinguishing features.

31 Marie Bonaparte, *Topsy: The Story of a Golden-Haired Chow*
    (London, 1994), p. 127.

32 Budiansky, *The Truth about Dogs*, pp. 20–22.

33 Donna Haraway, *The Companion Species Manifesto: Dogs, People
    and Significant Otherness* (Chicago, il, 2003), pp. 43–50.

34 Hearne, *Adam's Task*, p. 44.

35 Andrea Gullo, Unna Lassiter and Jennifer Wolch, 'The Cougar's Tale', in *Animal Geographies: Place, Politics and Identity in the Nature–Culture Borderlands*, ed. Jennifer Wolch and Jody Emel (London, 1998), p. 141.

36 Elizabeth Marshall Thomas, *The Hidden Life of Dogs* (Boston, MA, 1993), p. xiv.

37 *Ibid.*, pp. 36–7.

38 David Gordon White, *Myths of the Dog-Man* (Chicago, IL, 1991), p. 50.

39 Glen Elder, Jennifer Wolch and Jody Emel, '*Le pratique sauvage*: Race, Place and the Human–Animal Divide', in *Animal Geographies*, p. 73.

40 Serpell, *In the Company of Animals*, p. 66.

41 Teresa Mangum, 'Dog Years, Human Fears', in *Representing Animals*, ed. Nigel Rothfels (Bloomington, IN, 2002), p. 36; see also Kathleen Kete, *The Beast in the Boudoir: Petkeeping in Nineteenth-century Paris* (Berkeley, CA, 1994), pp. 81–6.

42 Kendall Crolius and Anne Montgomery, *Knitting with Dog Hair: Better a Sweater from a Dog You Know and Love than from a Sheep You'll Never Meet* (New York, 1997).

43 Schwartz, *A History of Dogs*, pp. 56–7.

44 Edward C. Ash, *Dogs: Their History and Development* (London, 1927), p. 5.

45 Josephine Diebitsch Peary, *My Arctic Journal: A Year among Ice-Fields and Eskimos* (New York, 1893), p. 42.

46 Doug O'Harra and Natalie Phillips, 'Wanted: Healthy, Happy Dogs', *Anchorage Daily News*, 12 February 2002, http://www.adn.com/iditarod/history/25/story/761862p-814679c.html

47 Coppinger and Schneider, 'Evolution of Working Dogs', p. 22.

48 Alan Beck and Aaron Katcher, *Between Pets and People: The Importance of Animal Companionship* (New York, 1983), p. 185.

49 William K. Powers and Marla N. Powers, 'Putting on the Dog: For the Oglala Indians, Canine Stew Is a Delicacy', *Natural History*,

xcv/2 (1986), pp. 8–11.

50 Marcie Griffith, Jennifer Wolch and Unna Lassiter, 'Animal Practices and the Racialization of Filipinas in Los Angeles', *Society and Animals*, x/3 (2002), pp. 234–5.

51 Freddie Farre, 'Letters: Dog-Eating in the Philippines', *Animal People Online* (2003), http://www.animalpeoplenews.org/03/6/letters6.03.html; see also Willie C. Cacdac, 'Dog Meat Eaters Warned of Double-Dead Canines', *Manila Times*, 29 May 2003, http://www.manilatimes.net/national/2003/may/29/prov/2003 0529pro5.html

52 Griffith, Wolch and Lassiter, 'Animal Practices', pp. 238–9.

53 James George Fraser, *The New Golden Bough*, ed. Theodor H. Gaster (New York, 1959), p. 533.

54 *Ibid.*, p. 517.

55 Powers and Powers, 'Putting on the Dog', p. 9.

56 Sophia Menache, 'Dogs: God's Worst Enemies?', *Society & Animals*, v/1 (1997), http://www.psyeta.org/sa/sa5.1/menache.html

57 Jeremy MacClancy, *Consuming Culture: Why You Eat What You Eat* (New York, 1992), p. 182.

58 Elder, Wolch and Emel, '*Le pratique sauvage*', p. 77.

59 Ann N. Martin, *Foods Pets Die For: Shocking Facts about Pet Food* (Troutdale, OR, 2003), pp. 17–27.

60 Dana Flavelle, 'Nibbles and Bits of Dogs, Cats and Sick Cows', *Toronto Star*, 18 July 2003, p. F4; see also William Lamb, 'Cats and Dogs Go to Landfills for Burial Now: Rendering Plant Stopped Accepting the Animals' Carcasses Last Month; Other Alternatives Are Weighed', *St Louis Post-Dispatch*, 16 January 2002, p. B1.

61 Ann Hodgman, 'No Wonder They Call Me a Bitch', in *The Best American Essays*, ed. Robert Atwan (Boston, MA, 2001), pp. 195–6.

62 Schwartz, *A History of Dogs*, p. 92.

63 White, *Myths of the Dog-Man*, pp. 71–2.

64 Menache, 'Dogs: God's Worst Enemies?'.

65 Schwartz, *A History of Dogs*, p. 23.

66 Corbett, *The Dingo*, p. 22.

67 Deborah Bird Rose, *Dingo Makes Us Human: Life and Land in an Australian Aboriginal Culture* (Cambridge, 2000), pp. 42–9.

68 Mary Miller and Karl Taube, *The Gods and Symbols of Ancient Mexico and the Maya* (London, 1993), p. 80.

69 Edith Hamilton, *Mythology: Timeless Tales of Gods and Heroes* (New York, 1969), p. 34.

70 White, *Myths of the Dog-Man*, pp. 176–7.

71 *Ibid.*, p. 159.

72 Patricia Dale-Green, *Lore of the Dog* (Boston, MA, 1967), p. 90.

73 Menache, 'Dogs and Human Beings'.

74 Dale-Green, *Lore of the Dog*, p. 98.

75 White, *Myths of the Dog-Man*, pp. 38, 228 n. 83, and 174.

76 Menache, 'Dogs: God's Worst Enemies?'.

77 Masson, *Dogs Never Lie*, p. 206.

78 Ronald Paulson, *Popular and Polite Art in the Age of Hogarth and Fielding* (Notre Dame, IN, 1979), p. 253, n. 5.

79 Dale-Green, *Lore of the Dog*, p. 94.

80 Iain Zaczek, *Irish Legends* (Dublin, 1998), p. 57.

81 Menache, 'Dogs: God's Worst Enemies?'.

82 Dale-Green, *Lore of the Dog*, pp. 144–5.

83 White, *Myths of the Dog-Man*, p. 125.

84 A radical is a standardized, component part of *kanji* (Chinese characters or ideograms) that makes indexing systems such as dictionaries possible. Most *kanji* have two or more radicals, usually considered that part of the character which is associated with its meaning. But these meanings became increasingly complicated after 1946, when radicals were simplified as part of the wider orthographic reform instituted by US occupying forces in Japan. Consequently, character etymology has become speculative, the subject of scholarly debate as well as a pastime popular among older men in Japan. See Mark Spahn and Wolfgang Hadamitzky, *Japanese Character Dictionary* (Tokyo, 1989), pp. v–viii.

85 Powers and Powers, 'Putting on the Dog', p. 7.

86 White, *Myths of the Dog-Man*, p. 13.

87 Paulson, *Popular and Polite Art*, p. 49.

88 William Empson, *The Structure of Complex Words* (New York, 1951), pp. 158–9.

89 White, *Myths of the Dog-Man*, pp. 63–4.

90 E. B. White, *One Man's Meat* (New York, 1944), p. 199.

91 Brian Vesey-Fitzgerald, *The Domestic Dog: An Introduction to Its History* (London, 1957), p. 163.

92 Boria Sax, 'What Is a "Jewish Dog"? Konrad Lorenz and the Cult of Wildness', *Society & Animals*, v/1 (1997), http://www.psyeta.org/sa/sa5.1/sax.html.

93 Lorenz, *Man Meets Dog*, p. 85.

94 Beck and Katcher, *Between Pets and People*, p. 238.

95 Colette Audry, *Behind the Bathtub: The Story of a French Dog*, trans. Peter Green (Boston, MA, 1963), p. 155.

96 *Ibid.*, p. 158.

97 J. R. Ackerley, *My Dog Tulip* (New York, 1987), pp. 149–50.

2 BREEDS

1 Raymond Coppinger and Richard Schneider, 'Evolution of Working Dogs', in *The Domestic Dog: Its Evolution, Behaviour and Interactions with People*, ed. James Serpell (Cambridge, 1995), p. 23.

2 Brian Vesey-Fitzgerald, *The Domestic Dog: An Introduction to Its History* (London, 1957), p. 33.

3 A. Croxton Smith, *British Dogs* (London, 1947), p. 45.

4 James Serpell, *In the Company of Animals: A Study of Human–Animal Relationships* (Cambridge, 1996), p. 259.

5 Benjamin L. Hart, 'Analysing Breed and Gender Differences in Behavior', in *The Domestic Dog*, p. 69.

6 Glenn Collins, 'Kennel Club Recalls Its Canine Bible after Outcry on Profiles', *New York Times*, 10 April 1998, p. A15.

7 M. B. Willis, 'Genetic Aspects of Dog Behavior with Particular Reference to Working Ability', in *The Domestic Dog*, pp. 61–2.

8 John Paul Scott and John L. Fuller, *Genetics and the Social Behavior of the Dog* (Chicago, IL, 1965), p. 389.

9 *Ibid.*, p. 407.

10 Serpell, *In the Company of Animals*, p. 17.

11 Edward C. Ash, *Dogs: Their History and Development* (London, 1927), p. 59.

12 Serpell, *In the Company of Animals*, p. 44.

13 Ash, *Dogs: Their History*, p. 63.

14 Vesey-Fitzgerald, *The Domestic Dog*, p. 75.

15 Ash, *Dogs: Their History*, p. 96.

16 Vesey-Fitzgerald, *The Domestic Dog*, p. 75.

17 Sophia Menache, 'Dogs: God's Worst Enemies?', *Society & Animals*, v/1 (1997), http://www.psyeta.org/sa/sa5.1/menache.html, characterizes these changes in terms of a shift from the anti-materialist doctrine of St Paul to the love for all creation advocated by St Francis of Assisi.

18 See Edward Said, *Orientalism* (New York, 1979), who defines 'orientalism' historically as a discourse, a specific language developed to denigrate Eastern societies by exoticizing them, that is integral to their colonization by Westerners, through which 'European culture gained in strength and identity by setting itself off against the Orient as a sort of surrogate and even underground self', p. 5.

19 Robin Gibson, *The Face in the Corner: Animals in Portraits from the Collection of the National Portrait Gallery* (London, 1998), p. 9.

20 Ash, *Dogs: Their History*, pp. 161–3.

21 Jean-Claude Schmitt, *The Holy Greyhound: Guinefort, Healer of Children since the Thirteenth Century* (Cambridge, 1983), pp. 124–5.

22 *Ibid.*, p. 46.

23 David Gordon White, *Myths of the Dog-Man* (Chicago, IL, 1991), p. 59.

24 Carson I. A. Ritchie, *The British Dog: Its History from Earliest Times* (London, 1981), claims pre-twelfth century evidence of the Guinefort legend, p. 52; Schmitt, *The Holy Greyhound*, documents its fifteenth-century currency in a letter featuring a crest with a greyhound in a cradle, p. 46.

25 Schmitt, *The Holy Greyhound*, p. 59.

26 Smith, *British Dogs*, p. 9.

27 Leon Rooke, *Shakepeare's Dog* (Toronto, 1985), p. 45; Vesey-Fitzgerald, *The Domestic Dog*, p. 76; and Ash, *Dogs: Their History*, p. 98.

28 Smith, *British Dogs*, p. 10; Ritchie, *The British Dog*, pp. 62–3.

29 Ash, *Dogs: Their History*, pp. 95–7.

30 *Ibid.*, pp. 193–7.

31 Sophia Menache, 'Dogs and Human Beings: A Story of Friendship', *Society & Animals*, vi/1 (1998), http://www.psyeta.org/sa/sa6.1/MENACHE.html

32 Sarah Orne Jewett, *The Queen's Twin and Other Stories* (Boston, 1899).

33 *The Irish Songbook*, ed. Joy Graeme (London, 1979), p. 102.

34 Donald Posner, *Watteau: A Lady at Her Toilet* (London, 1973), p. 80.

35 Richard Thomson, '"Les quat' pattes": The Image of the Dog in Late Nineteenth-century French Art', *Art History*, v/3 (1982), p. 329.

36 Marion Schwartz, *A History of Dogs in the Early Americas* (New Haven, CT, 1997), p. 133.

37 *Ibid.*, p. 35

38 Elsie P. Mitchell, *The Lion-Dog of Buddhist Asia* (Rutland, VT, 1991), p. 24.

39 Sophia Menache, 'Dogs and Human Beings'.

40 *A Medieval Home Companion: Housekeeping in the Fourteenth Century (Le ménagier de Paris)*, ed. and trans. Tania Bayard (New York, 1991), p. 53; see also Sophia Menache, 'Dogs and Human Beings'.

41 Ronald Paulson, *Popular and Polite Art in the Age of Hogarth and Fielding* (Notre Dame, IN, 1979), p. 54.

42 Vesey-Fitzgerald, *The Domestic Dog*, notes that Barner is commonly misidentified as a noblewoman, a member of the Berner family, p. 80.

43 Patricia Dale-Green, *Lore of the Dog* (Boston, MA, 1967), pp. 76–9.

44 Ash, *Dogs: Their History*, p. 78.

45 *Ibid.*, p. 83.

46 Miguel de Cervantes Saavedra, *Exemplary Stories*, trans. C.A Jones (Harmondsworth, 1972).

47 Steve Baker, *Picturing the Beast: Animals, Identity and Representation* (Urbana, IL, 2001), pp. xvii–xviii.

48 Geoffrey Chaucer, 'General Prologue', *The Riverside Chaucer*, ed. Larry Dean Benson (Boston, MA, 1987), p. 25.

49 Abraham Fleming, *Of English Dogges, the Diversities, the Names, the Natures and the Propensities* (Washington, DC, 1945), p. 2.

50 *Ibid.*, p. 20. See also Serpell, *In the Company of Animals*, p. 80, who cites William Harrison's paraphrasing of this passage, which was wrongly attributed by Harrison to Caius and not so explicitly misogynistic as Fleming.

51 Marjorie Garber, *Dog Love* (New York, 1996), p. 135.

52 Caroline Knapp, *Pack of Two: The Intricate Bond Between People and Their Dogs* (New York, 1998), pp. 186–8.

53 Marie Bonaparte, *Topsy: The Story of a Golden-Haired Chow* (London, 1994), pp. 71–2.

54 Gertrude Stein, 'Identity a Poem', in *The Stein Reader*, ed. Ulla E. Dydo (Evanston, IL, 1993), pp. 588-94.

55 Gertrude Stein, 'What Are Masterpieces and Why Are There So Few of Them' (New York, 1940). p. 84.

56 Lawrence K. Corbett, *The Dingo in Australia and Asia* (Ithaca, NY, 1995), p. 13.

57 Michael J. Rossi, *James Herriot: A Critical Companion* (London, 1997), p. 52.

58 Juliet Clutton-Brock, 'Origins of the Dog: Domestication and Early History', in *The Domestic Dog: Its Evolution, Behaviour and Interactions with People*, ed. James Serpell (Cambridge, 1995), p. 18; see also H. Epstein, *Domestic Animals of China* (Farnham Royal, 1969), p. 138.

59 Dale-Green, *Lore of the Dog*, pp. 128–9.

60 Harriet Ritvo, *The Animal Estate: The English and Other Creatures in the Victorian Age* (Cambridge, MA, 1987), p. 94.

61 Jonathan Burt, 'The Effect of Pets in the Nineteenth and Early Twentieth Centuries', in *Hounds in Leash: The Dog in Eighteenth-*

and Nineteenth-century Sculpture, ed. Jonathan Wood and Stephen Feeke (Leeds, 2000), p. 55.

62 Clifford L. B. Hubbard, *An Introduction to the Literature of British Dogs: Five Centuries of Illustrated Dog Books* (Aberystwyth, 1949), p. 41.

63 Vesey-Fitzgerald, *The Domestic Dog*, p. 143.

64 Ritvo, *The Animal Estate*, p. 96.

65 Dinks, 'The Sportsman's *Vade Mecum*', in *The Dog*, ed. Frank Forester (New York, 1873), p. 1.

66 Theo Marples, *Prize Dogs: Their Successful Housing, Management and Preparation for Exhibition from Puppyhood to the Show Ring* (Manchester, 1905), p. 11.

67 Robert Rosenblum, *The Dog in Art from Rococo to Postmodernism* (New York, 1988), p. 17.

68 Hal Opperman, *J.-B. Oudry, 1686–1755* (Seattle, WA, 1983), pp. 182–6.

69 Paulson, *Popular and Polite Art*, p. 53.

70 Ritvo, *The Animal Estate*, p. 93.

71 *Ibid.*, p. 115.

72 Thomson, '"Les quat' pattes"', p. 326.

73 Bruce McCall, Introduction, *Sit! The Dog Portraits of Thierry Poncelet* (New York, 1993), p. 1.

74 Garber, *Dog Love*, pp. 163–4.

75 Alan Beck and Aaron Katcher, *Between Pets and People: The Importance of Animal Companionship* (New York, 1983), p. 188.

76 Evan Watkins, *Everyday Exchanges: Marketwork and Capitalist Common Sense* (Stanford, CA, 1998), pp. 145–6.

77 Rosenblum, *The Dog in Art*, p. 67.

78 Teresa Mangum, 'Dog Years, Human Fears', in *Representing Animals*, ed. Nigel Rothfels (Bloomington, IN, 2002), p. 38; see also Marion Scholtmeijer, *Animal Victims in Modern Fiction: From Sanctity to Sacrifice* (Toronto, 1993), p. 45.

79 Kathleen Kete, *The Beast in the Boudoir: Petkeeping in Nineteenth-century Paris* (Berkeley, CA, 1994), p. 27.

80 Richard Ormond, *Sir Edwin Landseer* (New York, 1981), p. 94.

81 Robin Gibson, *The Face in the Corner*, p. 19.

82 Smith, *British Dogs*, p. 38.

83 Anna Snaith, 'Of Fanciers, Footnotes and Facism: Virginia Woolf's *Flush*', *Modern Fiction Studies*, XLVIII/3 (2002), p. 617.

84 Roger Grenier, *The Difficulty of Being a Dog*, trans. Alice Kaplan (London, 2000), p. 102.

85 Virginia Woolf, *Flush* (London, 1933), p. 78.

86 Clinton Sanders, *Understanding Dogs: Living and Working with Canine Companions* (Philadelphia, PA, 1999), p. 6.

87 Mangum, 'Dog Years', p. 41.

88 Gibson, *The Face in the Corner*, p. 57.

89 Garber, *Dog Love*, p. 21.

90 Dale-Green, *Lore of the Dog*, p. 44.

91 Susan McHugh, 'Video Dog Star: William Wegman, Aesthetic Agency and the Animal in Experimental Video Art', *Society and Animals*, IX/3 (2001), p. 231.

92 Knapp, *Pack of Two*, p. 24.

93 Beck and Katcher, *Between Pets and People*, p. 172.

94 *Ibid.*, p. 173.

95 Konrad Lorenz, *Man Meets Dog*, trans. Marjorie Kerr Wilson (Harmondsworth, 1964), p. 88.

96 Smith, *British Dogs*, p. 40.

97 Ash, *Dogs: Their History*, p. 98.

98 Paulson, *Popular and Polite Art*, pp. 57–8.

99 Baker, *Picturing the Beast*, p. 23.

100 Lars Eighner, *Travels with Lizbeth: Three Years on the Road and on the Streets* (New York, 1993), p. 135.

101 Vicki Hearne, *Bandit: Dossier of a Dangerous Dog* (New York, 1991), pp. 49–50.

102 Vesey-Fitzgerald, *The Domestic Dog*, p. 138.

103 Ritchie, *The British Dog*, p. 49.

104 L. S. Guggenberger, 'Dogs in Germany', *Nineteenth Century*, XXII (1887), p. 203.

105 Jilly Cooper, *Animals in War* (Guilford, CT, 2002), pp. 73–4.

106 Anna Waller, *Dogs and National Defense* (Washington, DC, 1958), p. 51.

107 Gary Genosoko, Introduction, *Topsy*, p. 27, n. 10.
108 Beck and Katcher, *Between Pets and People*, p. 172.
109 John E. O'Donnell, *None Came Home: The War Dogs of Vietnam*
     (Bloomington, IN, 2000), p. 181.
110 Barbara Bush, *C. Fred's Story* (Garden City, NY, 1984), p. 24.
111 E. B. White, *One Man's Meat* (New York, 1944), p. 183.
112 Vesey-Fitzgerald, *The Domestic Dog*, p. 151.
113 Sanders, *Understanding Dogs*, p. 56.
114 *Ibid.*, p. 57.

3 MUTTS

1 Zhang Chengzhi, 'Statue of a Dog', trans. Andrew F. Jones,
   Positions: East Asia Cultures Critique, X/3 (2002), p. 512.
2 *Ibid.*, p. 523.
3 Edward C. Ash, *Dogs: Their History and Development* (London,
   1927), pp. 116–20
4 Ronald Paulson, *Popular and Polite Art in the Age of Hogarth and
   Fielding* (Notre Dame, IN, 1979), p. 54.
5 *Ibid.*, p. 61.
6 Robert Rosenblum, *The Dog in Art from Rococo to Postmodernism*
   (New York, 1988), p. 43.
7 Richard Thomson, '"Les quat' pattes": The Image of the Dog in
   Late Nineteenth-century French Art', *Art History*, V/3 (1982), p. 331.
8 Roger Grenier, *The Difficulty of Being a Dog*, trans. Alice Kaplan
   (London, 2000), pp. 13–14.
9 Rosenblum, *The Dog in Art*, p. 10.
10 Thomson, '"Les quat' pattes"', p. 334.
11 Frederick Marryat, *Snarleyyow; or, The Dog Fiend* (Ithaca, NY,
    2000), p. 371.
12 Paul A. Gilje, *The Road to Mobocracy: Popular Disorder in New York
    City, 1763–1834* (Chapel Hill, NC, 1987), pp. 224–32.
13 Coral Lansbury, *The Old Brown Dog: Women, Workers and
    Vivisection in Edwardian England* (Madison, WI, 1985), p. 14.
14 [Margaret] Marshall Saunders, *Beautiful Joe* (New York, 1920), p. 1.

15 Teresa Mangum, 'Dog Years, Human Fears', in *Representing Animals*, ed. Nigel Rothfels (Bloomington, IN, 2002), p. 37.

16 John Muir, *Stickeen* (New York, 1915), p. 4.

17 *Ibid.*, p. 73.

18 Andrew C. Isenberg, 'The Moral Ecology of Wildlife', in *Representing Animals*, p. 52.

19 Jack London, *Call of the Wild*, ed. Daniel Dyer (Norman, OK, 1997), p. 71.

20 Gordon Korman, *No More Dead Dogs* (New York, 2000), p. 5; on the formulaic qualities of *Stickeen* and *Old Yeller*, see also Karla Armbruster, '"Good Dog": The Stories We Tell about Our Canine Companions and What They Mean for Humans and Other Animals', *Papers on Language & Literature*, xxxviii/4 (2002), pp. 351–76.

21 Alan Beck and Aaron Katcher, *Between Pets and People: The Importance of Animal Companionship* (New York, 1983), p. 209.

22 Millie Bush, *Millie's Book: As Dictated to Barbara Bush* (New York, 1990), p. 18.

23 *Ibid.*, p. 68.

24 Xaviera Hollander, *The Happy Hooker* (New York, 1972), p. 34.

25 Marjorie Garber, *Dog Love* (New York, 1996), p. 153.

26 Nadine Gordimer, *A World of Strangers* (New York, 1958), p. 96.

27 J. M. Coetzee, *Disgrace* (New York, 1999), p. 146.

28 Tommie L. Jackson, 'The Canine in Ngugi's *A Grain of Wheat* and Nadine Gordimer's *A World of Strangers*: A Metaphor for the Master–Slave Relationship between the Colonizer and the Colonized', *College Language Association*, XLV/2 (2001), p. 189.

29 Coetzee, *Disgrace*, p. 146.

30 Deborah Bird Rose, *Dingo Makes Us Human: Life and Land in an Australian Aboriginal Culture* (Cambridge, 2000), p 187.

31 Anita Desai, 'Diamond Dust', in her *Diamond Dust and Other Stories* (Boston, MA, 2000), p. 56.

32 Beck and Katcher, *Between Pets and People*, p. 235.

33 Paul Auster, *Timbuktu* (New York, 1999), p. 158.

34 John Berger, *King: A Street Story* (New York, 1999), p. 187.

35 Lars Eighner, 'Lizbeth', in *Living with the Animals*, ed. Gary Indiana (Boston, MA, 1994), p. 18.

36 *Ibid.*, pp. 14–16.

37 Clinton Sanders, *Understanding Dogs: Living and Working with Canine Companions* (Philadelphia, PA, 1999), p. 135.

38 Melanie Rehak, 'A Roof of One's Own: Questions for Lars Eighner', *New York Times Magazine*, 7 March 1999, national edn, section 6, p. 23.

39 Eighner, *Travels with Lizbeth: Three Years on the Road and on the Streets* (New York, 1993), p. 71.

40 Garber, *Dog Love*, p. 93.

41 Eighner, *Travels with Lizbeth*, pp. 209–12.

42 Franz Kafka, *Selected Short Stories of Franz Kafka*, ed. and trans. Willa Muir and Edwin Muir (New York, 1993), p. 270.

43 Gilles Deleuze and Félix Guattari, *Kafka: Toward a Minor Literature*, trans. Dana Polan (Minneapolis, MN, 1986), pp. 17–18.

4 DOG FUTURES

1 Patricia Dale-Green, *Lore of the Dog* (Boston, MA, 1967), p. 164.

2 Glen Elder, Jennifer Wolch and Jody Emel, '*Le pratique sauvage*: Race, Place and the Human–Animal Divide', in *Animal Geographies: Place, Politics and Identity in the Nature–Culture Borderlands*, ed. Jennifer Wolch and Jody Emel (London, 1998), p. 75.

3 Read Bain, 'The Culture of Canines: A Note on Subhuman Sociology', *Sociology and Social Research* (1928), p. 551.

4 *Ibid.*, p. 555.

5 John Paul Scott and John L. Fuller, *Genetics and the Social Behavior of the Dog* (Chicago, IL, 1965), p. vi.

6 James Serpell and J. A. Jagoe, 'Early Experience and the Development of Behaviour', in *The Domestic Dog: Its Evolution, Behaviour and Interactions with People*, ed. James Serpell (Cambridge, 1995), p. 80.

7 Scott and Fuller, *Genetics*, p. 397.

8 Alan Beck, *The Ecology of Stray Dogs: A Study of Free-Ranging Urban*

    Animals (Baltimore, MD, 1973) p. xii.

9 *Ibid.*, pp. 63–5.

10 *Ibid.*, p. 55.

11 C. Fred Bush, *C. Fred's Story*, ed. Barbara Bush (Garden City, NY, 1984), p. 11.

12 Alan Beck and Aaron Katcher, *Between Pets and People: The Importance of Animal Companionship* (New York, 1983), p. 186.

13 Donna Haraway, *Simians, Cyborgs and Women: The Reinvention of Nature* (London, 1991), p. 190.

14 Donna Haraway, *The Companion Species Manifesto: Dogs, People and Significant Otherness* (Chicago, IL, 2003), p. 16.

15 'Project Goals', *The Missyplicity Project*, http://www.missyplicity.com

16 James W. Humphreys, Jr, 'Humans in Space: Medical Challenges', in *Space: National Programs and International Cooperation*, ed. Wayne C. Thompson and Steven W. Guerrier (London, 1989), pp. 133–4.

17 Marjorie Garber, *Dog Love* (New York, 1996), pp. 72–3.

18 Jeffrey Moussaieff Masson, *Dogs Never Lie about Love: Reflections on the Emotional World of Dogs* (New York, 1998), p. 183.

19 Garber, *Dog Love*, p. 71.

20 Tim Radford, 'Fate of First Canine Cosmonaut Revealed', *The Guardian*, 30 October 2002, http://www.guardian.co.uk/space-documentary/story/0,2763,822214,00.html

21 Clyde R. Bergwin and William T. Coleman, *Animal Astronauts: They Opened the Way to the Stars* (Englewood Cliffs, NJ, 1963), p. 17.

22 Transcript, *Partners of the Heart*, PBS Online, http://www.pbs.org/wgbh/amex/partners/filmmore/pt.html

23 National Research Council, *Dogs: Standards and Guidelines for the Breeding, Care and Management of Laboratory Animals* (Washington, DC, 1973), p. 28.

24 Jean Bethke Elshtain, 'Why Worry about the Animals?', *Progressive*, LIV/3 (1990), pp. 17–18.

25 H. G. Wells, *The Island of Dr Moreau* (London, 1988), p. 52.

26 Henrietta Mondry, 'Beyond Scientific Transformation in

Bulgakov's *The Heart of a Dog'*, *Australian Slavonic and East European Studies*, x/2 (1996), pp. 5–6.

27 Kathleen Cook-Horujy and Avril Pyman, trans., *The Heart of a Dog and Other Stories* (Moscow, 1990), pp. 306–7.

28 Mikhail Bulgakov, *Heart of a Dog*, trans. Mirra Ginsburg (New York, 1968), p. 120.

29 Steve Baker, *Picturing the Beast: Animals, Identity and Representation* (Urbana, IL, 2001), p. 71.

30 J.R.R. Tolkien [John Ronald Reuel], *Roverandom*, ed. Christina Scull and Wayne G. Hammond (New York, 1998), p. 51.

31 Scull and Hammond, Introduction, *Roverandom*, p. xix.

32 'Disturbing Scenes of Death Show Capability with Chemical Gas', *CNN Online*, 19 August 2002, http://www.cnn.com/2002/US/08/19/terror.tape.chemical/

33 National Research Council, *Dogs: Standards and Guidelines*, p. 44.

34 Romesh Ratnescar and Douglas Waller, 'Did al Qaeda Do This?', *Time*, Online edition, 18 August 2002, http://www.time.com/time/world/article/0,8599,338577,00.html

35 Konrad Lorenz, *Man Meets Dog*, trans. Marjorie Kerr Wilson (Harmondsworth, 1964), p. 97.

36 Steve Baker, *Picturing the Beast: Animals, Identity and Representation* (Urbana, IL, 2001), p. 109.

37 Jonathan Goldberg in *Sodometries: Renaissance Texts, Modern Sexualities* (Stanford, CA, 1992) notes that as the US was building an international coalition to support the first Gulf War, a *Rolling Stone* magazine t-shirt ad sold a bizarre picture of Saddam Hussein's face superimposed on the anus of a camel with the surrounding text 'America will not be Saddam-ized', equating the Iraqi invasion of Kuwait as well as all acts of forced entry with sodomy. The complicities of racism, homophobia and xeno-phobia that long ago led Europeans to disavow sodomy as 'the vice of Mediterranean / Islamic cultures' are now, hundreds of years later, working in this t-shirt ad to support a war effort between modern nation-states, pp. 1–3. While the camel signals regional conflict, later associations with dogs depict Hussein as a

global threat.

38 Baker, *Picturing the Beast*, pp. 115–16.

39 Robert Fisk, 'The Human Cost: "Does Tony Have any Idea what the Flies Are Like that Feed Off the Dead?"', *The Independent*, Online edition, 26 January 2003, http://news.independent.co.uk/world/politics/story.jsp?story=3 72767

40 James Serpell, 'The Hair of the Dog', in *The Domestic Dog*, p. 262.

41 Baker, *Picturing the Beast*, p. 85.

42 Haraway, *The Companion Species Manifesto*, p. 12.

Bibliography

Ackerley, J. R., *My Dog Tulip* (London, 1956)

American Kennel Club, *The Complete Dog Book: The Photograph, History and Official Standard of Every Breed Admitted to AKC Registration, and the Selection, Training, Breeding, Care and Feeding of Pure-bred Dogs* (New York, 1997)

Audry, Colette, *Behind the Bathtub: The Story of a French Dog*, trans. Peter Green (Boston, MA, 1963)

Auster, Paul, *Timbuktu* (New York, 1999)

Ash, Edward C., *Dogs: Their History and Development* (London, 1927)

Beck, Alan, *The Ecology of Stray Dogs: A Study of Free-Ranging Urban Animals* (Baltimore, MD, 1973)

Berger, John, *King: A Street Story* (New York, 1999)

Bulgakov, Mikhail, *The Heart of a Dog*, trans. Mirra Ginsburg (New York, 1968)

Caius, Johannes, *De canibus Britannicus* (London, 1570)

Coetzee, J. M., *Disgrace* (New York, 1999)

Coppinger, Raymond, and Lorna Coppinger, *Dogs: A New Understanding of Canine Origin, Behavior and Evolution* (Chicago, IL, 2001)

Corbett, Lawrence K., *The Dingo in Australia and Asia* (Ithaca, NY, 1995)

Coventry, Francis, *The History of Pompey the Little; or, The Life and Adventures of a Lap-dog* (London, 1773)

Crolius, Kendall, and Anne Montgomery, *Knitting with Dog Hair: Better a Sweater from a Dog You Know and Love Than from a Sheep*

You'll Never Meet (New York, 1997)

Dale-Green, Patricia, *Lore of the Dog* (Boston, MA, 1967)

Edwards, Sydenham, *Cynographia Britannica* (London, 1800–05)

Eighner, Lars, *Travels with Lizbeth: Three Years on the Road and on the Streets* (New York, 1993)

Fleming, Abraham, *Of English Dogges, the Diversities, the Names, the Natures and the Propensities* (London, 1576)

Garber, Marjorie, *Dog Love* (New York, 1996)

Grenier, Roger, *The Difficulty of Being a Dog*, trans. Alice Kaplan (London, 2000)

Haraway, Donna, *The Companion Species Manifesto: Dogs, People and Significant Otherness* (Chicago, IL, 2003)

Hearne, Vicki, *Bandit: Dossier of a Dangerous Dog* (New York, 1991)

Hubbard, Clifford L. B., *An Introduction to the Literature of British Dogs: Five Centuries of Illustrated Dog Books* (Aberystwyth, 1949)

Kennel Club, *The Kennel Club's Illustrated Breed Standards: The Official Guide to Registered Breeds* (London, 2003)

Knapp, Caroline, *Pack of Two: The Intricate Bond Between People and their Dogs* (New York, 1998)

Knight, Eric, *Lassie Come-Home* (New York, 1940)

Lawick, Hugo von, *Solo: The Story of an African Wild Dog*, intro. Jane von Lawick-Goodall (Boston, MA, 1974)

Layard, Daniel Peter, *An Essay on the Bite of a Mad Dog* (London, 1763)

London, Jack, *The Call of the Wild* (New York, 1903)

Lorenz, Konrad, *Man Meets Dog*, trans. Marjorie Kerr Wilson (Harmondsworth, 1964)

Marryat, Capt. Frederick, *Snarleyyow; or, The Dog Fiend* (Philadelphia, PA, 1837)

Mitchell, Elsie P., *The Lion-Dog of Buddhist Asia* (Rutland, VT, 1991)

Muir, John, *Stickeen* (New York, 1909)

Ouida [Louise de la Ramée], *A Dog of Flanders, and Other Stories* (London, 1872)

Ritchie, Carson I. A., *The British Dog: Its History from Earliest Times* (London, 1981)

Rose, Deborah Bird, *Dingo Makes Us Human: Life and Land in an*

Australian Aboriginal Culture (Cambridge, 2000)

Rosenblum, Robert, *The Dog in Art from Rococo to Postmodernism* (New York, 1988)

Sanders, Clinton, *Understanding Dogs: Living and Working with Canine Companions* (Philadelphia, PA, 1999)

Saunders, [Margaret] Marshall, *Beautiful Joe* (Philadelphia, PA, 1893)

Schmitt, Jean-Claude, *The Holy Greyhound: Guinefort, Healer of Children since the Thirteenth Century* (Cambridge, 1983)

Schwartz, Marion, *A History of Dogs in the Early Americas* (New Haven, CT, 1997)

Scott, John Paul, and John L. Fuller, *Genetics and the Social Behavior of the Dog* (Chicago, IL, 1965)

Serpell, James, ed., *The Domestic Dog: Its Evolution, Behaviour and Interactions with People* (Cambridge, 1995)

Stables, Gordon, *Sable and White: The Autobiography of a Show Dog* (London, 1893)

Steinbeck, John, *Travels with Charley, in Search of America* (New York, 1962)

Terhune, Albert Payson, *Lad: A Dog* (New York, 1919)

Thomas, Elizabeth Marshall, *The Hidden Life of Dogs* (Boston, 1993)

Tolkien, J.R.R. [John Ronald Reuel], *Roverandom*, ed. Christina Scull and Wayne G. Hammond (New York, MA, 1998)

Vesey-Fitzgerald, Brian, *The Domestic Dog: An Introduction to Its History* (London, 1957)

Wegman, William, *Man's Best Friend* (New York, 1982)

—, *Puppies* (New York, 1997)

White, David Gordon, *Myths of the Dog-Man* (Chicago, IL, 1991)

Woolf, Virginia, *Flush: A Biography* (London, 1933)

Youatt, William, *On Canine Madness* (London, 1830)

Associations

AMERICAN KENNEL CLUB (AKC)

http://www.akc.org/
The American Kennel Club, a non-profit organization established in 1884, maintains a pure-bred dog registry, sanctions dog events and promotes responsible dog ownership. In 2002 it registered almost 1,000,000 dogs.

CANID SPECIALIST GROUP (CSG)

http://www.canids.org/index.htm
The CSG is the world's chief body of scientific and practical expertise on the status and conservation of all canid species, advising the Species Survival Commission (SSC) of the World Conservation Union (IUCN), based in Switzerland. It publishes the scientific journal *Canid News*.

NATIONAL SERVICE DOG CENTER OF THE DELTA SOCIETY

http://www.deltasociety.org/dsb000.htm
The NSDC is a web-based program that provides information and resources for people with disabilities. It also provides information for people who are interested in training or donating a puppy for service.

DOG WRITERS ASSOCIATION OF AMERICA (DWAA)

http://www.dwaa.org/
Founded in 1935, the DWAA began as an organization of reporters, editors and publishers to secure press facilities at large dog shows. Now it also encourages writing about canine companionship and sport through award programmes, competitions, scholarships and a newsletter.

KENNEL CLUB

http://www.the-kennel-club.org.uk/
The Kennel Club was established in Britain in 1873 to serve as a controlling body to regulate dog shows and trials. One of its first projects was to compile and maintain the Stud Book, the standard of most canine pedigrees today. Now registering more than 200,000 dogs annually, its mission has expanded to promote the general improvement of dogs. It publishes *Kennel Gazette*.

NATIONAL CANINE DEFENCE LEAGUE

http://www.ncdl.org.uk
Provides care and welfare for stray, abandoned and unwanted dogs and for dogs whose owners have died. Finds new owners where possible. There are various centres across the UK.

BATTERSEA DOGS HOME

http://www.dogshome.org.uk
Cares for unwanted dogs and strays, and for dogs whose owners have died. Finds new owners where possible. There are homes at London (Battersea), Berkshire (Old Windsor) and Kent (Brands Hatch).

Websites

Many dog-related sites go up and down on the web each day. Because most are commercial and breed-specific, the following list is limited to sites devoted to commemorating individual dogs, promoting non-profit dog-related organizations and maintaining reliable links to similar sites.

Dogcam, a link from the main page of the Lost Dog's Home and Cat Shelter (the third largest animal shelter in Australia), has easily downloadable digital film clips from the perspective of dogs wearing cameras: http://www.lostdogs.com.au/dogcam/

Scroll down the *Dogs on the Web* site (maintained by Dick Neville) to the general list, which is one of the most comprehensive and regularly updated collections of links to dog-related websites: http://www-hsc.usc.edu/~rneville/doglinks.html

How to Love Your Dog is, as the subtitle says, *A Kids' Guide to Dog Care*, created and maintained by Janet Wall (a teacher for 23 years) as an interactive educational tool for children: http://www.kidsanddogs.bravepages.com/

Lars Eighner regularly updates the *Lizbeth Memorial*, a site that honours the dog who spent several years on the road and on the streets with him: http://www.io.com/~eighner/lizpics.html

Acknowledgements

I am deeply grateful to everyone who has helped me to research, write and illustrate this book. I especially want to thank: Jonathan Burt, Michael Leaman, Harry Gilonis, Robert Williams, CoryAnne Harrigan, Deborah Mix, Stephanie Turner, Gabrielle Schueler, Brendan Devlin, Kathleen Maloney, Nigel Rothfels, Steve Baker, Richard Dienst, Siobhan Somerville, Vincent Leitch, Arkady Plotnitsky, Brandy Walker, Tabitha Sparks, Stacy Takacs, Ron Broglio, Alan Rauch, Carol Senf, Jennifer Wheelock, Anouar Majid, Jaime Hylton, Jennifer Tuttle, David Kuchta, Joseph Mahoney, Paddy Hall, Ali Ahmida, Elizabeth de Wolfe, Linda Sartorelli, Ron Morrison, Denise Gendron, Andrew Abalahin, Tim Guttman, Alexandra Campbell, Matthew Anderson, Jacque Carter, John Tumiel, Robert Haskell, Martha Grenon, Sidney Harris, Daphne Hereford, Mark Hughes, Thierry Poncelet, Serge Poulin, Yves Sebille, Vladimir Semenov, William Wegman, Martin Whelan, Alfred Wood, Andi Zeisler, Andrea Feldman, Holly Haywood, Kelly Moore, Barbara Kolk, Janice Beal, Barb Swartzlander, Cally Gurley, Bridin and Padraic Connelly, Alice Smith, George McHugh, Bridget Kusior, Maura Stockford McHugh, my parents Ed and Eileen McHugh, and most of all Mik Morrisey, to whom this book is dedicated.

The dogs who have helped are legion. For them I thank all dogs.

Photo Acknowledgements

The author and publishers wish to express their thanks to the below sources of illustrative material and/or permission to reproduce it. (Some sources uncredited in the captions for reasons of brevity are also given below.)

Arthur M. Sackler Museum (Harvard University Art Museums), Cambridge, Mass. (gift of Charles A. Coolidge), photo Michael A. Nedzweski, © 2004 President and Fellows of Harvard College: p. 69; reprinted from Edward Ash, *Dogs: Their History and Development* (London, 1927), pp. 60, p. 93 (foot), p. 110 (foot); British Library, London (photos © British Library Reproductions): pp. 13, 36, 45, 53, 110 (top) (ADD. MS. 42130), 169; British Museum, London: p. 134; The Samuel Courtauld Trust, Courtauld Institute of Art Gallery, London: p. 100; photo © Dell Comics/Random House: p. 120 (foot); photo: © 2003 Brendan Devlin: p. 101; photo courtesy Dungarvan Museum (www.dungarvanmuseum.org), © 2003 Martin Whelan: p. 78; photo Bob Greene/© Paramount Pictures: p. 107; photos Doane Gregory and Wren Maloney, © 2000 Warner Bros.: p. 102; collection of the Grunwald Center for the Graphic Arts, UCLA Hammer Museum, Los Angeles (anonymous gift): p. 131; © 2003 Sidney Harris (www.science-cartoonsplus.com): p. 10; photos Holly Haywood: pp. 19, 25, 30, 86; photo © 2003 Daphne Hereford (www.rintintin.com): p. 120 (top); © 2003 Mark Hughes/The Vermont Cartoon Factory, Burlington, Vermont (www.vermontcartoonfactory.com): p. 180 (top); reproduced from the Institute of Laboratory Animal Resources Subcommittee on

Index